PATHMASTER GUIDES

CIRCULAR 30 WALKS FROM REGIONAL CENTRES

THE ITALIAN LAKES

Richard Sale

Series Editor
Richard Sale

The Crowood Press

First Published in 1992 by
The Crowood Press Ltd
Ramsbury
Marlborough
Wiltshire SN8 2HR

British Library Cataloguing in Publication Data
A catalogue record for this book is
available from the British Library

Picture credits
All photographs by the authors; except for Cascata del Toce, by Marina Tirelli; all maps by Sharon Perks.

Acknowledgements
The authors would like to thank all their friends - Italian and English - who have accompanied them on the hills.
They offer sincere thanks to Monica Neroni for all her considerable efforts in assisting with the translation.
Richard Sale would also like to thank the many people in Italy who have made him welcome on his trips, most especially Francesco Milone in Como and Giacomo Carioli in Stresa, and would also like to thank Alberto Fasola for occasional assistance in making conversations involving poor Italian and poor English more intelligible.

In places, times from timetables and certain costs, including fares, have been quoted. These were correct at time of going to press, but it cannot be guaranteed that they will remain the same in subsequent years.

Typeset by Carreg Limited, Nailsea, Bristol
Printed and bound in Great Britain by
BPCC Hazells Ltd
Member of BPCC Ltd

CONTENTS

Introduction   5

The Walks

    Lakes Maggiore and Orta   27
    Lakes Lugano and Como   63
    From Lake Como to Lake Garda   115
    Lake Garda   128

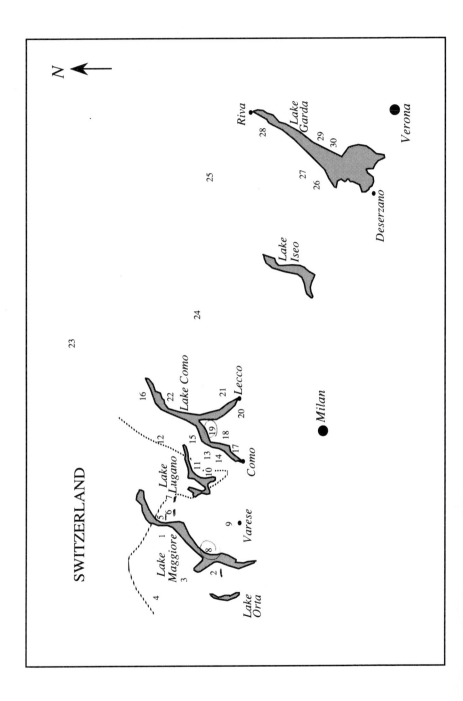

SWITZERLAND

N

Lake
Maggiore

Lake
Orta

Lake
Lugano

Varese

Lake Como

Como

Lecco

Milan

Lake
Iseo

Riva

Lake
Garda

Deserzano

Verona

1
2
3
4
5
6
7
8
9
10
11
12
13
14
15
16
17
18
19
20
21
22
23
24
25
26
27
28
29
30

INTRODUCTION

The Italian Lakes as a Walking Area

Alexander Dumas, arriving at Lake Maggiore after crossing the Simplon Pass, noted that "the sky is pure, the air mild, and one recognises the land beloved of the gods, the happy land that neither barbarous invasions, nor civil discords could deprive of its heaven-sent blessings".

That the comment was made about Lake Maggiore rather than Lake Como or Lake Garda is irrelevant. The sentiments would, I am sure, have been the same had Dumas arrived at either of those lakes, or at any of the others. Though famed as a tourist area - and Dumas' comments would support that fame - the area is equally good for the walker. The high ridges that define the valleys now filled by the lakes are lower than those of the high alps to the north, but that makes them easier of access. There is also another advantage: from the walks in this book the view includes not only the high peaks, but the lakes themselves, all of which are extremely photogenic.

During the Pleistocene era of geological time, at the time of the Quaternary Ice Age, it was not rivers, but glaciers that flowed south from the high Swiss-Italian Alps towards what is now the Po Plain. These glaciers were confined by the ridges of hard rock that still define the northern valleys, gouging out the bottoms of those valleys and depositing, as terminal and lateral moraine, the material they removed. The over-deepening of the valleys, and the thickness of the morainic deposits, produced deep basins that filled as the glaciers retreated, leaving huge lakes of fresh water bounded by rich bands, of soil that separated them both from their confining ridges, and the Po Plain. The depth of both the lakes and the moraine deposits are impressive. Lake Garda, for example, is 346 metres (1135 feet) deep, the moraine deposits contributing 149 metres (484 feet) to that depth. The lake's deepest point lies 281 metres (922 feet) below sea level.

Lake Garda, though not unique in this thickness of morainic deposit, is slightly unusual, because the deposit's thickness allows it to extend far out of its valley into the plain. Alone of the lakes, Garda has almost a third of its length beyond the end of its confining ridges. In common with the others, however, its more northerly end is confined by high ridges, the lakes pushing northward into the Alps so far that they have an almost fjord-like appearance at their extreme northern tips. The best example of this is Como, whose northern end is not only fjord-like, but shows quite spectacularly the V-formed cross-section of ridges that is such a characteristic of glacial valleys.

The confining mountains of the lakes change as we go from Lake Garda in the east, westward towards Lake Maggiore. Initially the rock is calcareous, first of all being the dolomitic limestone that gives the peaks their name, the Dolomites. Ironically for a mountain area that is so famously characteristic of Italy, the name derives from that of a French geologist, Dolomieu, who first identified this magnesium-rich rock. As we go westward there are occasional intrusions of crystalline rocks, the intrusions becoming more frequent until by the time we reach Lake Maggiore the mountains - strictly the pre-Alps, rather than the Alps themselves - are wholly crystalline, a mixture of schists and gneisses. This change of rock type changes the vegetation and its profusion. The most obvious change is in the woods, the abundant, and apparently ubiquitous, chestnut trees in fact growing only where the crystalline rocks intrude.

In general the western area has a more varied and luxuriant growth, but this really only applies to the upland areas. Near the lakes the growth is governed by the deposition of the lateral and terminal moraine, with Garda's considerable deposits giving its shorelines a richness that the other lakes can barely match.

How to Get There

By Air

The Italian Lakes are served by Milan's two International airports. Linate is situated adjacent to the city's orbital autostrada almost due east of the city centre. At Linate flights land from all the main European cities together with Italian internal flights. Malpensa lies to the east of Gallarate, about 14 kilometres (9 miles) from the "Busto Arsizio" exit of the A8 autostrada. This is the intercontinental airport with flights from all over the world, including New York, Montreal and Toronto. Both Linate and Malpensa are connected to Milan's Central Station by bus.

Venice's Marco Polo Airport - connected to all main European airports - could also be used, especially if Lake Garda was the destination.

Orio sul Serio, Bergamo's airport, and Villafranca, Verona's airport, are situated beside the A4 autostrada. Increasingly, these airports are being used by charter flights from British airports.

By Rail

Central Station, Milan is connected to all leading European cities, mostly by overnight sleeper trains. There is an Information Centre at the station open 7am to 11pm every day including Sunday. Central Station is on Metro Lines 2 (green) and 3 (yellow) and is served by a number of buses and trams.

Porta Garibaldi Station is connected by motorail link to Paris and Boulogne. From Britain all-in tickets are available for ferry/train journeys. This service is not cheap, but it is huge adventure for children and does cut out the long haul across Europe, thus adding several days to your holiday. The trip leaves Boulogne in mid-afternoon, passes Paris in the early evening, goes through the Simplon Tunnel while you are asleep and deposits you for a free breakfast in Porta Garibaldi at about 6am.

A second motorail service runs through the Simplon tunnel, cars loading and off-loading at each end of the tunnel. This service will be of interest to those driving down through Switzerland as it allows the car to be put on the train at Kandersteg, in the Bernese Oberland, or at Brig in the Valais. The former avoids having to drive around the Oberland ridge, but the latter is of more debateable merit, as the traveller saves little time and very few miles, those he does save being through some of the finest of rock-gorge scenery.

By Road

Travelling from within Italy the area of the northern lakes is easily reached by the excellent autostrada system that uses Milan as a hub. From outside Italy the alpine chain must be breached, the most popular routes through being the Mont Blanc Tunnel or Great St. Bernard Pass to the Aosta Valley; the Simplon Pass from Brig in Switzerland to Domodossola and Lake Maggiore; the St. Gotthard and St. Bernardino Passes to Bellinzona and Lakes Maggiore, Lugano and Como; the Spluga Pass from Chur, the Maloja and Bernina Passes from St. Moritz, and the Ponte del Gallo and Stelvio Passes into the Valtellina; and the Brenner Pass from Austria into Trentino and the north tip of Lake Garda.

Please remember that all autostrada are toll roads.

Those travelling to Italy in their own cars should note that they are eligible to receive petrol coupons from the ACI (Italian Automobile Club) offices at the border crossing into the country. The coupon booklet contains vouchers for the lire equivalent of about 150 litres of fuel. The booklet offers a discount of about 20% on pump prices and has two other advantages. Firstly a toll card is included for use on automatic autostrada booths, amounting to a toll total of about 30,000 lire, and possession of the booklet makes the owner a temporary member of ACI so that its emergency services can be called upon. These include free car hire if your car breaks down and will be off the road for more than 12 hours. If you do need the service ring 116, or ask for ACI at the autostrada SOS columns - situated every 2 kilometres ($1^1/_4$) miles) along the carriageway.

To obtain a booklet the visitor must be in a foreign car, not in a rented Italian car, and must be able to show his car's registration certificate.

The speed limits on Italian roads are:-

Engine Capacity	Autostradas	All Other Roads
Cars up to 1099cc Motor Cycles 150-349cc	110 km/h (68mph)	90 km/h (56mph)
Cars over 1100cc Motor Cycles over 350cc	130 km/h (80mph)	100km/h (62mph)
Other Vehicles	90 km/h (56mph)	80 km/h (50mph)

In all built-up areas the speed limit is 50 km/h (31mph). It is advisable to keep to these limits: fines are on-the-spot and non-negotiable.

To drive in Italy you must have a green card insurance certificate, the vehicle's registration certificate, the owner's written permission if the vehicle is not yours and a translation of your British driving licence - available from British motoring organisations.

Italian traffic regulations require the wearing of seat belts and the carrying of a warning triangle.

Terrain and Climate

The terrain covered by the walks in the book varies from wooded valley through grassed hillside - alp or alpine pasture - to bare, rocky slope. In the walk description the type of terrain is mentioned, though it is best to assume that all of the walks will involve some sections of rough going.

In summer the lakes' area is hot and sunny - not for nothing is it a tourist area ! - and the walker should expect lake level temperatures of 25-30°C (77-86°F) and, on occasions, even higher. In winter many of the upland areas are winter sport resorts - it will be cold and the ground may well be snow covered, or icy.

Accommodation

As might be expected of a tourist area, the Italian Lakes have a wide range, and an abundance of accommodation. The range extends from Cernobbio's Villa d'Este, one of Europe's finest hotels where one night will cost as much as a month's camping fees, to camp sites.

All the major towns and villages have small tourist hotels. Lists are available at the local tourist offices, from where bookings can be made.

Camping is popular with walkers, and also with the Italians. All of the lakes have sites, but the density varies from sparse (Lake Como) through entirely adequate (Lake Maggiore) to overwhelming (Lake Garda). The sites are star-rated - the system comparable to other European countries - and lists are available from tourist offices or from :-

Centro Internazionale Prenotazioni Federcameggio
Casella Postale 23
50041 Calenzano
Firenze
Tel: 055 882391

The Italian Youth Hostel Association has limited accommodation near the lakes. Contact the address below for details:

Associazone Italiana Alberghi per la Gioventu
Palazzo della Civiltà del Lavoro
Quadrato della Concordia
00144 EUR Roma
Tel: 06 5913702

Transport

Railways

Milan is connected by rail to Lake Maggiore, to Varese (by the private Ferrovia Nord as well as the state railway), to Como (again by Ferrovia Nord as well as the state rail service) and to Bergamo, Brescia and the southern tip of Lake Garda, all of which are on the line to Venice.

The eastern shore of Lake Orta, and the western shore of Lake Maggiore as far as the river Toce, are served by lines that meet at Cuzzago in the Val d'Ossola before crossing into Switzerland via the Simplon tunnel.

The remainder of Lake Maggiore's western shore has no railway, though a line runs continuously along the eastern shore from Sesto Calende into Switzerland.

Lake Lugano is not well served by rail, though a line from Varese does terminate at Porto Ceresio, and one from Como goes to Capolago and along the lake to Lugano, having crossed the lake bridge.

On Lake Como the only railway line runs from Lecco up the eastern shore, before serving the length of the Valtellina. A line runs up Lake Iseo's eastern shore and on up Val Camonica, but none of the Lake Garda towns, apart from Desenzano and Peschiera, are served by rail.

Lake Steamers

Despite there now being very few steamers on the lakes, the word is still used to cover the variety of passenger boats that daily criss-cross the waters of the larger lakes - Orta, Maggiore, Lugano, Como, Iseo and Garda. Chiefly the services are modern diesel ferry boats, with a number of the decidedly more exciting hydrofoils (aliscafo) that reduce crossing times for a price supplement that is, in general, about 50%. To take advantage of their speed the hydrofoils do not call at all ports, taking more direct lines between the lake ends.

Price reductions are also available for those who buy "season" tickets, tickets being available for one day, several days, one or two weeks. The diesel and hydrofoil ferry services, together with the car-ferries that offer limited crossings, and then only on the three major lakes, are scheduled services operating every day. In addition the steamer companies run special services in the summer months, offering sight-seeing tours, together with excellent night-time trips on light-bedecked boats with dancing to live music. Some of these trips are by "old-fashioned" paddle steamer, offering an unforgettable outing, particularly when the trip passes close to some of the floodlit highlights of the lakes, the Rocca d'Angera on Lake Maggiore and Malcesine's castle on Lake Garda to give just two (excellent) examples. The boats for these trips have restaurants and bars, full air-conditioning, and the best of sound systems.

Lake Orta

There is a limited service on the smallest of the big lakes, linking Omegna, Pettenasco, Orta S Giulio and Pella, a full round trip taking about $1^{1}/_{2}$ hours. In addition a boat service links Isola S Giulio with Orta S Giulio in just a few minutes.

Lake Maggiore

There is a full service on Lake Maggiore linking Arona, Angera, Meina, Lesa, Belgirate, Stresa, Carciano, the Borromean Islands, Baveno, Verbania-Pallanza, Villa Taranto, Intra, Laveno, Ghiffa, Porto Valtravaglia Oggebbio, Cannero, Luino, Maccagno and Cannobio, continuing to Brissago, Porto Ronco, Ranzo, Gerra, Ascona, S Nazzaro, Vira, Magadino and Locarno, all in Switzerland. In addition there are small local services linking Carciano and Verbania-Pallanza with the three Borromean Islands and the Villa Taranto. Because the service crosses the national border between Italy and Switzerland, a border that zig-zags across the water in curious style in order to stay in the middle of the lake and make right-angles with the shore, the services include customs and border officials, and passports must be carried and duty-payable goods must be declared.

The journey from Arona to Locarno and back takes about six hours if the outward journey is aboard the normal ferry, with its restaurant service, and the return by hydrofoil.

The lake's only car-ferry links Verbania-Intra with Laveno, the crossing taking around 20 minutes.

Lake Lugano

There is a full ferry service on the lake, an end-to-end journey having the additional delight of numerous crossings into and out of Switzerland. The formalities noted above for Lake Maggiore also apply here.

The ferry links Ponte Tresa, Lavena, Figino (Switzerland) and Porto Ceresio, crossing into Switzerland to reach Morcote, Brusino Arsizio, Melide, Poiana, Capolago, Bissone, Campione (Italy), Paradiso, Lugano, Castagnola, Caprino and Gandria, and crossing back into Italy to visit S Margherita, S Mamete, Claino-Osteno and Porlezza.

Lake Como

Diesel and hydrofoil ferries link a very large number of ports on Como's shores, particularly on the Como arm, and the western shore of the Colico arm. Como itself is a terminus, and from it ferries visit Tavernola, Cernobbio, Blevio, Moltrasio, Torno, Urio, Carate, Loglio, Faggeto Lario, Pognana Lario, Toriggia, Careno, Nesso, Brieno, Argegno, Colonno, Sala Comacina, Lezzeno, Lenno, Tremezzo, Cadenabbia and Bellagio. Continuing to Lake Colico, as the upper arm of Lake Como is sometimes called, the ferries reach Menaggio, Varenna, Bellano, Acquaseria, Rezzonico, Dervio, Cremia, Pianello del Lario, Musso, Dongo, Gravedona, Domaso, Gera Lario, Colico and a terminus at Piona. In the Lecco arm of the lake the ferries leave Bellagio for Lierna, Limonta, Oliveto, Mandello del Lario, Abbadia Lariana and finish at Lecco. In addition boats cross to Isola Comacina from several ports on the mainland close to the island.

A trip from Como to Piona, via Bellagio, and return, will take about six hours, more if Bellagio itself and the Abbey of Piona are visited. Such a trip can take advantage of the restaurants on the ferries and would be quicker if full advantage was taken of the hydrofoil service.

As an alternative to the ferry for sightseeing, Lake Como also has a flying boat service, regular tourist flights taking off from the lake close to the city of Como.

Lake Como has four car ferries criss-crossing the waters near Punta Spartivento, beyond Bellagio. They link Menaggio with Bellagio and with Varenna, and Cadenabbia with Bellagio and with Varenna. Each crossing takes from 15 to 30 minutes.

Lake Iseo

On Lake Iseo, ferries leave the Sarnico terminus for Clusane, Predore, Iseo, Sulzano, Tavernola Bergamasca, four ports on Monte Isola - Sensole, Siviano, Carzano and Peschiera Maraglio, - Sale Marasino, Marone, Riva di Solto, Castro, Lovere and Pisogne.

Some idea of the size of one of the smallest northern lakes is gained by realising that a full round trip, including a visit to Monte Isola, takes about 4 hours.

Lake Garda

On the largest lake there is, again, a full service of diesel and hydrofoil services, with restaurants and bars, and the full range of additional steamers offering day and night-time cruises.

Desenzano is the terminus for Garda steamers, and from it the ferries visit Sirmione, Peschiera del Garda, Lazise, Bardolino, Garda, Salo, Gardone Riviera, Fasano, Maderno, Torri del Benaco, Gargnano, Brenzone, Assenza, Malcesine, Limone sul Garda, Torbole and Riva sul Garda, with occasional boats calling at Manerba and Moniga, south of Salo, from Sirmione. A round trip from Desenzano to Riva and return would take around 6 hours.

In addition, there is a single car ferry service, from Maderno to Torri del Benaco, the crossing taking about 30 minutes.

Telephone Numbers for Lake Steamer Offices

Como	031 273342 or 260234
Garda	030 9141321
Iseo	035 971483
Lugano	091 515223
Maggiore	0322 46651 or 2352
	0323 30393, 42321 or 503220
Orta	0322 844862

Money

The Italian unit of currency is the lira (plural lire) with a change rate of around 2,000 to the £Sterling. Thankfully, the lira is not sub-divided.

Banks and change shops (cambio, wechsel) are open from 8.30am to 1.30pm and 3pm to 4pm. All banks will issue cash against major credit cards, though it is possible that the branch you choose does not have this facility.

Most major credit cards are taken by most hotels, restaurants and shops - look for the stickers in the windows. The major exceptions to this rule are garages which will accept cash only, or vouchers. Things are changing however.

Eurocheques are also taken at most hotels, restaurants and shops, but again there is reluctance in garages. Here too, though, a change is taking place.

The Law for Walkers

Italy is a very good country for walking, most of the adult population of the north of the country being outdoor enthusiasts who take full advantage of their beautiful outdoors. Each town, and a good many of the villages have their own branch of the CAI (Club Alpino Italiano - Italian Alpine Club) and, probably, their own mountain hut (rifugio) in which the club members stay at weekends. A rifugio will not only have beds, but will serve coffee, and wine, and meals, though these may be fairly basic. For information on all such mountain huts, and for details of temporary membership, contact:-

Club Alpino Italiano
Via Foscolo 3
Milan
Tel: 02 802554 or 8057519

In addition to their preparations for their weekend comfort the club members waymark footpaths throughout their areas. The waymarking consists, at the worst, of paint splashes applied to trees or rocks, at best to signs with route numbers erected at strategic points. Unfortunately the signing is always to the local group footpath numbering scheme, there being no overall system. This means that to follow the routes successfully you must be in possession of a walking map of the area. In addition some of the areas publish guides to their routes, though these are only available in Italian, and do not show the routes, except as line drawings.

With all these advantages the walker should be able to avoid trespass. The Italian trespass law is straightforward: access is allowed to all unfenced land, but is denied to all private land. As the majority of walks in this book follow marked paths, or start on high ridges, above the private land 'limit', few problems should be experienced.

Italy has no code for walkers, but the standard courtesies - drop no litter, light no fires, pick no flowers and do not disturb wildlife - are expected of everyone.

Clothing and Equipment

The country covered by the walks is high, but in an area of high ambient temperature where the cooling effect of altitude is not always as much as might be expected. The problem is, therefore, that the walker may start out on a hot day and perspire heavily and then may, or may not, reach an area where the temperature is lower and where there is a strong wind. It is therefore advisable to carry a windproof outer shell. Since thunderstorms are also possible - as we are in an area where cool alpine area is frequently meeting hot "Mediterranean" air - the windproof shell should ideally be waterproof. Many will not relish the prospect of carrying a heavy waterproof shell (either a breathable such as Gore-tex or a lighter PU proof nylon) and may prefer one of the new generation windproofs which are only showerproof but very light. Karrimor's older stock "Climaguard" comes to mind, as do several of the newer materials. For the rest, it is worth taking a fleece jacket as the warmth on top of the hill will warrant the weight carried up it. Lightweight polycotton trousers will do, with, perhaps, a polycotton top. Many will find a hat of some sort useful to keep the sun off the head. Sunglasses are also handy, many of the walks being set among rocks and rock faces which, since the usual colour of the rock is white, act as mirrors and increase glare.

On the feet boots are essential. Many of the routes use mule tracks which are uneven and prone to being covered with ankle-turning rocks. A twisted ankle, or worse, should be avoided at all costs, many of the walks being in (relatively) remote areas. Ankle support from the boots is therefore vital. If you are used to going out in reasonable walking shoes and are happy that they give you sufficient support then they will probably be OK, but do be sure before setting off.

The above notes are for the Summer (or late Spring/early Autumn) walker. If you plan to go in Winter, bear in mind that you will have less daylight to complete a walk, and that the country may be snow or ice covered, and the temperature at or below (even well below) freezing. Be adequately equipped.

A map and compass should always be carried, as should some food and drink. The British walker will find the heat and altitude trying and may dehydrate quickly. Take fluid at every available opportunity: it will help to delay the onset of fatigue and cramp each of which is accelerated by dehydration. Since altitude has been raised, it is worth pointing out that few of the walks presented here go high enough for oxygen debt to produce anything more noticeable than an increased heart rate for normal speed climbing or walking, or a slightly increased heart rate recovery time at stops. Walk 4 goes highest by some margin, reaching 2,980 metres ((9,774 feet) at which height oxygen debt is definitely noticeable. On that route, take your time: acclimatisation in a few hours is not possible, but you can relatively quickly come to terms with what is, or is no longer, possible.

Apart from Walk 21A which is very specific in terms of equipment - dealt with in the introduction to that walk - nothing special is needed. One or two of the walks use a section of chain to overcome a steepish rock step, but these require neither special equipment or special skills.

Food and Wine

It will come as no surprise to discover that the local specialities are fish dishes, the lakes and their feeding rivers holding a variety of coarse fish which are served in ways seemingly without number. The most popular fish are trout and perch, the preferred servings being with herbs or soused. For something very different try the missoltini, sun-dried fish.

Away from the lakes the mountain areas specialise in the serving of salted meats - try the spit-roasted salted mutton, perhaps with a few slices from a big, round, dark brown rye loaf - sausages and dairy products. The sausages are, chiefly, polenta, a maize-based pudding, often served flavoured, with rabbit or the mountain fungi for which the areas are also famous, or with the Italian delicacy currently under fire from conservationists - song birds. The Ossola valley near Lake Maggiore is famous for its viulin, leg of goat salted and stuffed with herbs and spices. Nearby, in Val Vegezzo, S. Maria Maggiore is famous for its smoked ham. The Valtellina, near Sondrio, is more famous for its dried salted beef, while the Valganna, near Varese, has its own risotto. Try, too, the gnocchi, a pasta of white and chestnut flour, mashed potato and pumpkin, with bread-crumbs and egg-yolk, seasoned with nutmeg and the local area's secret spice recipe.

Many of the valleys have there own cheese specialities, the best known being Taleggio from the valley of the same name that links the Val Brembana and the Valsassina, to the north of Bergamo, but try also the goat's cheese of the Brianza, south of Lake Como. Many, also, have honey in numerous flavours, assisted by the profusion of alpine flowers, azaleas and rhododendrons.

To wash the local dishes down there are the local wines. Italy has a huge number of wines, usually drunk locally since they do not travel well. Since there is no very specific naming system some caution must be exercised, occasionally quite disparate wines having the same names. Usually it is best to look for labels that refer to the government's grading system. The lowest grade - DS, for Denominazione Semplice - has no quality standard. DOC, Denominazione di Origine Controllata, wines meet defined quality standards and come from officially recognised production areas. DCG, Denominazione Controllata & Garantita, wines are of the highest standards.

Well-known wines from Novara, the region that includes the western shore of Lake Maggiore, are Barolo and Barbaresco, dry, full-bodied red wines, and Asti Spumante, the sparkling white. Lombardian wines tend to be white from the plains - Moscato and Reisling dell'Oltepro Pavese - and red from the mountains - the famous Valtellina wines, Sassella, Grumello and Inferno. Lake Garda is famous for three wines, the full-bodied, red Valpolicella, the lighter red, dry Bardolino, and the dry white Soave.

In addition there are many distilled spirit drinks, most famously those sold at Piona Abbey at the northern tip of Lake Como, but also those from other mountain areas, distilled from alpine herbs and wild fruits such as strawberries and bilberries.

In bars, particularly those in the bigger towns, to obtain coffee or a drink the procedure is to pay for what you want at the cashier who will issue you with a ticket that you take to the counter. There the "waiter" will ask you to repeat your order, check your ticket and serve your drink. It usually costs a little extra to sit down, both inside and outside. And speaking of coffee, traditional Italian coffee (liscio) is served in very small cups, is thick and black, usually heaped with sugar by Italians, and is lethal in any quantity.

There is, apparently, a stronger version called ristretto. If that is true then bars selling it should carry a health warning.

If you wish to prolong enjoyment, life or both, then go for a longer version. Café Lungo is served with hot water, café macchiato with a little milk. Cappucino, vernacularly called cappucio is served with a frothed milk and occasionally topped with chocolate powder. It is usually drunk at breakfast, and asking for it during the day will evoke glances that assess your virility.

Preparations Before You Go

A current passport is all that is needed to get into Italy.

As Italy is a member of the EEC, the visitor from Britain need only carry a form E111 - available from the Department of Health and Social Security - to obtain free medical treatment. If drugs are prescribed these will be dispensed at a pharmacy (*farmacia*) and a small, non-reimbursible, local tax will be payable.

Visitors from outside the EEC should check the validity of their personal health insurance before travelling.

The maps given in this book are not intended to be definitive. Rather they are to enable you to locate and follow the route on your own map of the area. For each walk the relevant Kompass map sheet is given. These maps, at 1:50,000, cover the whole of the area covered by the book, but are not the only maps to do so. The Tabacco maps, also at 1:50,000, cover the area equally well and also carry footpath information. Some areas also have local maps at larger scales, usually published by CAI, or in conjunction with the local tourist offices. Ask at the offices if you wish to carry a larger scale map.

Health Hazards

The major health hazard for the walker in the Lakes area is the sun, especially as the walks usually involve a great deal of climbing. In an attempt to reduce the risk, the times for the walks are longer than would be anticipated if the walk was in a more temperate country. Some walks will appear to have very long times and will produce a sceptical response from the reader. Try one first. Not until you have zig-zagged up a 1,200 metre (about 4,000 foot) climb at high angle, to a finishing altitude of around 2,000 metres (about 6,500 feet) in a temperature in the low eighties will you be able to compare your time against the book time and to adjust them accordingly.

The grades are more difficult to justify as they are personal and because they attempt to include factors that are matters of opinion as well as fact. Thus if a walk takes the walker over rough, exposed terrain deep into high mountain country is that walk easy if it takes only 3 hours? By the same token is a straightforward walk with few and easy gradients close to civilisation with numerous refreshment points difficult if it takes around 7 hours to complete? Many would argue the exact reverse - in terms of grade - to be the truth and would be able to construct an entirely reasonable case in support of that assertion. The grades given attempt to iron out these problems, hopefully making due allowance for required effort, terrain, commitment, time, etc. If you disagree with a grade we can only apologise.

Finally, whatever you think about the grades wear, or take, a hat.

One last hazard which is frequently mentioned in books on northern Italy is snakes. It is true that there are several poisonous snakes local to the area, but the chances of seeing one, let alone being bitten, are slight. If it should happen, stay as calm as possible and seek immediate medical assistance.

A Brief History

The area's fertility was noted early, in the wake of the glaciers that had carved the lake basins retreating as the Ice Age ended, and immediately exploited. The very early Bronze Age Remedello culture is named for the earliest known site, near Brescia, and there are also other very early sites, chiefly pile dwellings, at the edges of several of the smaller lakes. Later, Iron Age, peoples also moved into the area, though the most famous of these, the Etruscans, are commemorated by the regional name Tuscany, to the south of our area. While the Etruscan civilisation was flowering Romulus founded Rome - legend has it that this was in 753BC - so that its first governors were Etruscans rather than Romans. These early Romans, that is Etruscans living in and near Rome, were defeated in Northern Italy around 400BC by Gauls who swept across the Alps to found Cisalpine Gaul, Cisalpine meaning no more than "this side of the Alps". It was to be more than a century before true Romans, having rebuilt Rome following conquest by the Gauls, and having defeated Carthage in the Punic Wars, reconquered Northern Italy as the Roman Empire expanded.

Surprisingly, the lakes' area has very sparse Roman remains, those at Brescia, dating from the 1st century AD being about the best, though there are some isolated pieces at other places. In part, the reason for this is the conversion of the Roman Empire to Christianity, and the replacement of pagan temples with Christian churches on the same sites. The Emperor Nero had presided over the first persecution of Christians in 64AD, a persecution that lasted for 250 years, the last, and greatest, being under Diocletian in 303AD. The persecutions failed to reverse the tide of religious history, the tide washing ever faster following the Edict of Milan in 313AD when Constantine the Great granted religious freedom to the Empire's Christians. In 391AD Theodosius made Christianity the religion of the state. The same reasoning for the apparent lack of Roman remains also explains, in part, the lack of very early Christian remains, later churches having been built on the sites of earlier ones. Some of the best preserved treasures from the early Christian era can also be seen at Brescia, in the Christian Museum.

Ironically those two emperors, Constantine and Theodosius, assisted the fragmentation of the empire and, at the same time, laid the foundation for later Italian greatness. In 330AD Constantine moved the capital of the Empire to Byzantium, renaming it Constantinople, and in 395AD Theodosius divided the Empire into eastern and western halves. The link with the east that followed the transfer of power had profound implications for the Italian city states in the early Middle Ages, while the division of the Empire made the plundering of the western half by the northern barbarians easier, though it is almost certainly true that this plunder would have happened at some later stage even if there had been no division. The names of the "barbarians at the gates" have come down to us as household words for the atrocious - Huns and Vandals - but they also included one group who named the province within which almost the whole area of this book falls, the Longobards or Lombards. The origin of these people are not absolutely clear, though their route to Italy, across the Alps from the Danube basin, suggest somewhere around Hungary. They were pagan, but not really the barbarians of legend, having some impressively modern ideas - it is no coincidence that Lombard Street is the home of London's bankers.

Legend has it that the Lombards invaded Italy as a direct result of an invitation by one of the Emperor's senior officials at Constantinople. This man, Narses, was a eunuch who was deeply offended when the Emperor's wife suggested that rather than join in the defence of Constantinople he should join the women and spin wool, since he was no real man. Outraged, Narses sent Alboin, king of the Lombards, a case of fine northern Italian wine, with a suggestion that he should invade the poorly protected country of origin.

The Lombards were converted to Christianity by Theodolinda, the daughter of a Bavarian duke who married the Lombard king, and for this act of conversion Pope Gregory III sent her a True Nail, which was incorporated into - some say that, miraculously, it was beaten and, expanding, formed the whole of - an iron crown, which was thereafter used to crown the kings of Lombardy and, later, Italy. Both Charlemagne in the 8th century, and Napoleon in the 19th century were crowned with the Iron Crown, as were more than 40 kings in the 1000 years between those two. Today the Iron Crown can be seen at Monza Cathedral a little way north-east of Milan.

Charlemagne had defeated the Lombards in 794 taking the area into his Frankish Kingdom, but the Lombards had retaken the crown by the 8th century following the disruptions caused by the invasion of the Magyars of Hungary who plundered the whole of northern Italy. One King, Lothar, defeated and killed by Berengar, king of Ivrea, left a widow, Adelheid, who appealed for help to the German Emperor Otto, a plea that was answered by invasion. Berengar was defeated, Otto married Adelheid, was crowned Emperor in Rome, and began three centuries of German rule of the majority of Italy. This time was important for the rise of the Italian city states, and also for conflict between the papacy and the Emperors for overall control of the country.

The struggle between Pope and Emperor was given voice by struggles between noblemen supporting either the pro-Pope "Guelfs" or the pro-Emperor "Ghibellines", these two "party" names often being encountered on museum visits, though neither having any direct bearing on Italian cultural or, ultimately, political history. The same can most definitely not be said about the rise of the city states. The towns of northern Italy were at the cross-roads of the civilisations of the west and the east, on the pilgrimage routes to Rome and, most importantly, on the routes of the Crusades that kept the kings and noblemen of Europe active for many years around the 12th century. Venice, Pisa and Genoa arose as ports, growing rich on trade from the east and on the transportation of soldiers. Milan and, though later, Florence grew rich on their position, Milan in the fertile Po valley on trade routes inland from Genoa and Venice, Florence on the trade route to Rome. To us Venice is a magical city, how much more so it must have seemed to a yeoman crusade soldier from the agricultural countries north of the Alps.

From earliest times the cities were controlled not by feudal lords, but by elected councils of rich merchants: Venice's Doge was an elected official, more mayor than duke. These councils encouraged innovations in agriculture and expanded markets in every possible direction. Feudalism required few innovations, power was maintained by keeping the peasants down, but the merchants of the city states wanted increased efficiency and trade because that brought wealth. Marco Polo was a Venetian, and Leonardo Fibonacci, who brought Arabic numerals to Europe to replace the cumbersome Roman system, was Pisan. Later, when the city states were at the height of their power their wealth encouraged art: Dante was born in Florence in 1265 and a century later the same city saw the work of Donatello. By the 15th century the Renaissance had created perhaps the finest artistic climate that has ever existed at any time, anywhere, with Michelangelo, Leonardo, Raphael and Titian all alive and working at the same time, and Palladio designing buildings that still inspire awe. The work of these masters make any visit to northern Italy worthwhile because although only a limited amount of their work is visible, the effect of their presence on contemporaries and pupils is frequently seen.

It would be wrong, however, to believe that the rise and domination of the city states was painless. There was frequent inter-city rivalries: Florence fought Pisa, Genoa fought Venice. Milan fought Como in the Ten Years War, from 1118 to 1127, destroying that city. Aided by Emperor Frederic I known as Barbarossa - red beard - Como rose again, destroying the Island of Comacina in revenge and assisting the Emperor against Milan. At first the Emperor was successful, but the city states combined to form the Lombard League defeating Barbarossa at Legnano in 1176 and winning significant concessions in the Treaty of Constance in 1183.

Later some of the cities succumbed to lordships, though these remained, chiefly, benign. The Viscontis ruled Milan at first, later being replaced by the Sforzas, while the castles of Verona's Scaligeri family will be seen in almost every town on Lake Garda's shore.

Elsewhere in Italy at this stage the influence of the eastern states was declining. The Normans invaded Sicily and southern Italy around the same time as they were invading England. Indeed the ties between the two countries at this stage are remarkable: Hugh Grandmesnil fought with William at Hastings, but his son Robert became Abbot of a Calabrian monastery. French influence was destroyed following the "Sicilian Vespers" in 1282 when all Frenchmen were murdered and expelled, the House of Aragon that succeeded them supplying Emperors for the Holy Roman Empire and ensuring Spanish domination of much of Italy - Charles V's son, Philip II, was given Milan in 1540 and it remained a Spanish colony for 150 years.

Eventually the divided nature of Italy and the smallness of the city states meant that the country was open for attack by foreign powers. Not all of the business acumen of the cities failed however, in 1768 Genoa sold Corsica to France! By then, indeed 50 years before then as far as Lombardy was concerned, much of northern Italy had fallen under the rule of the Austrian Hapsburgs. Napoleon briefly freed the area, but declared himself king of Italy and replaced Hapsburg rule with small republics - the Cisalpine covering much of Lombardy, the Ligurian around Genoa - under the umbrella of France. When Austrian rule was re-established Italians began to awaken to the fact that they had a national identity and that they could throw off foreign rule. A real voice was given to this awakening by the appearance of a newspaper *Il Risorgimento* in Turin in 1842. Its title was taken up by the disparate groups fighting for unity and freedom: Carlo Alberto, the Piemontian King of Sardinia, Count Camillo Cavour, from Piemonte, an ardent monarchist, Giuseppe Mazzine, an anti-monarchist from Genoa, and Giuseppe Garibaldi, an enigmatic, but effective, guerilla leader. With help from France, most particularly at the battles of Magenta and Solferino, much of northern Italy was freed from Austrian rule and voted, with the remainder of mainland Italy, for unity with Sardinia, and for monarchy. In 1861 Vittorio Emanuele II, son of Carlo Alberto, was crowned King of Italy. Under his kingship war with Austria incorporated Venice into Italy, and the 1914-18 war added the South Tirol and Istria, apart from the city of Fiume.

Sadly, following the 1914-18 war the expansionist policy that had unified the country and brought the return of Italia Irredenta - Unrecovered Italy - continued. Mussolini's fascists took over the government, Annunzio took Fiume, Abyssinia and Albania were invaded, the "Pact of Steel" with Hitler came into being. Despite Mussolini's attempts at mediation the latter brought Italy into the war with France and Britain in June 1940. In 1943 Italy changed sides, the fascists were routed and, later, Mussolini was shot, but in the Treaty of Paris Italy lost Istria to Yugoslavia. In 1946 King Vittorio Emanuele III abdicated and a national referendum abolished the monarchy. Today Italy is a respected member of the European Economic Community, and of NATO.

Economically Italy is a country of staggering contrast. In the north the standard of living is as high as in any country in Western Europe while in the south it is almost the equal of any economic low spot. This is, in part, due to the groundwork of the medieval free city states, in part to the climate which is more amenable to agriculture in the north than it is in the very hot south, and in part due to the existence in the north of hydro-electricity and natural gas in a country that is, in general, chronically short of indigenous power sources. Milan, with a population of almost 2 million, is Italy's second biggest city behind Rome, but is the country's undoubted economic capital. Its shops, its fashion houses, its restaurants, everything about it, are the equal of any other European city, and in addition its artistic and architectural interest are considerable. Lombardy as a whole - Italy's fourth biggest region, with Milan as regional capital - is equally rich, and since virtually the whole of the area covered by this book lies in that region, the visitor can expect the highest standards, and will not be disappointed. The next door region of Piedmont, with its capital of Turin, is one of the three, with Sardinia and Sicily, that are larger than Lombardy and is equally rich.

Neither region, however, and the same is also true of Veneto and Trentino - Alto Adige to the east, relies on its wealth alone to attract the visitor. All are of considerable artistic interest, of virtually unsurpassable scenic beauty - particularly the area of the lakes - and have a climate that is enviable. All in all there can be few more attractive areas to spend a holiday.

Further Information

Telephones

Almost all the telephones in towns have now been converted to boxes that take both coins and phone cards. In all the new ones a red light at the top left of the call box will light if the machine is out of service. The machine coin boxes will, as a rule, take 100, 200 and 500 lire coins as well as gettone, tokens made specifically for telephones, available at kiosks, but more rarely seen nowadays. Phone cards are available in 5,000 and 10,000 lire values. The cards are available from kiosks and bars, and also from vending machines in the airports, stations and other large centres. The vending machines take notes and coins. Once you have obtained your card tear off the top left corner, as indicated, and it ready for use. Insert it into the slot on the card reader and wait for the current value to be indicated on the digital screen before dialling. The screen will count the value down for you as your call progresses. If the card runs out during the call you will hear the same warning tone that you hear when your money is running low, but there is a difference - when the card becomes empty of credit you cannot continue with the call by inserting coins, neither have you the time to insert another card. The call will terminate. If at the end of your call your card remains in credit, it will be returned automatically. Be patient, it only feels like the machine has eaten it out of spite.

For many the thought of using a foreign phone system is daunting. If this is the case, what you need is a SIP office. SIP is the national Italian phone company and in all major towns and cities they have offices in which there are individual booths. Tell the counter staff if you are intending to ring back to Britain as some of the booths only offer local calls. When you are given your booth you dial as usual and the price is displayed on a screen in front of you. At the end of the call you pay at the counter.

In addition many bars show a telephone symbol that indicates that they have a phone that you can use. Here you will be able to dial yourself, the price being registered at the counter where you will pay after. Sometimes, but not always, there will be a booth and a screen to tell you how much the call is costing. Sometimes the phone will just be in the bar and will have no read-out. But beware of talking up to the limit of your call: the bar is entitled to add a surcharge for the service so it will cost you more than is registered.

To obtain an international call dial 00. The code for Britain is 44, as it is from any other country in the world. Remember that when you dial you must leave off the 0 of the British STD code. Thus, to dial the Italian State Tourist Office in London (tel: 071 408 1254) from Milan - or anywhere else in Italy - you dial 00.44.71.408.1254

The following are numbers which hopefully you will never need:-

Police	113
Carabinieri	112
Fire Service	115
Ambulance	7733

For Emergency Service Ring 113. For immediate attention at airports, railway stations or hospitals, look for the sign PRONTO SOCCORSO

Public Holidays

January 1
January 6 (Epiphany)
Easter Sunday and Monday
April 25 (Liberation Day, 1945)
May 1
August 15 (Ferragosto)
November 1 (All Saints)
Christmas Day and Boxing Day

Useful Addresses

British Consulate
7 Via S. Paolo
Milan
Open 9am-12, 2.30pm-4.30pm Daily except Saturday
Tel: 02-803442 (02-862490 at nights and during holidays)

Italian State Tourist Office
1 Princes Street
London W1R 8AY
Tel: 071-408-1254

Tourist Offices in Italy

Most of the lakeside towns and the majority of the larger mountain villages have tourist/accommodation offices, but the main provincial offices (the APT office) are -

Novara   - 2, Corso Cavour   Tel: 0321 27238

though for information on the sections of Lakes Orta and Maggiore that lie in Piedmont it is worth contacting the offices at -

Orta S. Giulio	- 26, Piazza Motta	Tel: 0322 90355
Stresa	- 3, Piazzale Europa	Tel: 0323 30150
Varese	- 5, Piazza Monte Grappa	Tel: 0332 283604/ 284454
Como	- 17, Piazza Cavour	Tel: 031 274064
Bergamo	- 4, Via Vittorio Emanuele	Tel: 035 242226
Brescia	- 36, Corso Zanardelli	Tel: 030 45052
Sondrio	- 28, Piazza Garibaldi	Tel: 0342 214461

The chief office for Lombardian Tourism, which is also the Milan city office, is

Milan   - 1 Via Marconi   Tel: 02 809662
beside the cathedral (the Duomo)

The chief Veneto office near to Lake Garda, which is also the Verona city office, is

Verona   - 20 Via Carmelitani Scalzi Tel: 045 8000065
though for Lake Garda itself it is advisable to contact the local village offices, chief of which is at

Malcesine   - Palazzo dei Capitanai   Tel: 0451 600044

The chief Trentino office, which also the Trento city office, is

Trento   - 132 Corso 3 Novembre   Tel: 0461 980000/ 895111 though for Lake Garda itself it is advisable to contact the local village offices, chief of which is at

Riva del Garda - Palazzo dei Congressi Tel: 0464 54444

Italian Automobile Club (A.C.I.)

Head Office:	8, Via Marsala 00185 Rome Tel: 06-4998
Regional Offices:	16 Via A. Maj Bergamo Tel: 035-247621
	16 Via 25 Aprile Brescia Tel: 030-40561
	79 Via le M. Masia Como Tel: 031-556755
	12 Via A. De Gasperi Domodossola Tel: 0324-2008
	43 Corso Venezia Milan Tel: 02-7745
	36 Via Rosmini Novara Tel: 0321-30321
	12 Via Milano Sondrio Tel: 0342-212213
	6 Via Pozzo Trento Tel: 0461-25072
	25 Via le Milano Varese Tel: 0332-265150

THE WALKS

Lake Maggiore and Lake Orta

One of the most perceptive, comments ever made about Lake Maggiore was that of Stendhal, who arrived in the area in the wake of Napoleonic troops who had come, in 1800, to destroy the castle at Arona. Stendhal wrote, "When one, by chance, has a heart and a shirt, one should sell one's shirt to see the surroundings of Lake Maggiore".

Maggiore - the name means large, but refers to the length, Maggiore being longer than Lake Garda, but smaller in surface area - is a squiggle of a lake, its northern region lying in the Swiss canton of Ticino, its western shore lying in Piedmont, its eastern shore in Lombardy. The lake covers 215 square kilometres (84 square miles) and is 65 kilometres (41 miles) long, varying in width from 2 kilometres ($1^1/_4$ miles) at Angera in the south, to about 4 kilometres ($2^1/_2$ miles) in the central section, just south of Luino. In this central section the lake is also at its deepest, 372 metres (1220 feet) deep.

The lake, also known as the Verbano, from the original Roman name, is fed by two main rivers, the Ticino entering at the northern end and traversing the lake, in name at least, to become the only outflow at Sesto Calende. The second river, the Toce, flows into the square Borromean Bay, from the Val d'Ossola. In addition there are other rivers, draining the Pennine and Lepontine Alps, and the Tresa, that drains Lake Lugano, flows into Maggiore at Luino.

Lake Maggiore, as with the other lakes was glacially formed, the glaciers of the Quaternary Era gouging out valleys that already existed between the high alpine ridges, over-deepening them - all the big Italian lakes are extremely deep - and carrying down the material - the terminal moraine - that blocked off the outflows. By contrast Lake Mergozzo, that lies about $1^1/_2$ kilometres (1 mile) from the extreme tip of Maggiore's Borromean Bay, was formed in an entirely different way. Here sediments brought down by the river Toce were deposited on the shallow plain the river crossed before entering the lake, eventually building up to dam off the river which swung around Monte Orfano to follow the course we see today.

For the walker, the lake's shores become more interesting the further north he goes. This is not surprising, the glacier that formed the lake having developed from the high hills, but pushed the terminal moraine that blocked the southern end right out on to the Lombardy Plain. To the north-west are the high hills of the side valleys of Val d'Ossola, the walking being the better the further the walker goes from the lake. That is to imply that there is nothing close to the water worth considering. Such is not the case, as our walks above Lake Mergozzo and on the Mottarone above Stresa show. However we do give into temptation once, visiting the high Val Formazza to see what many consider to be Europe's most beautiful waterfall, the Cascata del Toce, as well as to see alpine snow in very close close-up. By complete contrast there is a much warmer walk between two of the lake's tourist resorts - though the start of this walk is reached by lake steamer.

On the opposite side of the lake there are beautiful valleys and high ridges close to the Swiss border. Several of our walks visit this area, meandering between Switzerland and Italy, while another uses the best funivia on any lake to reach the fine high point above Laveno for the start of a downhill walk back to the lakeside.

None of the walks in this section actually take the hilly ground around Lake Orta, but that is because all lists must stop somewhere, and should not be taken as implying that the lake is not worth the visit.

Lake Orta is filled by numerous streams draining down from the mountains that make the bowl in which it sits, and is itself drained by the Strona river that flows into the Toce at Gravellona Toce, and from there into Lake Maggiore. That means that the lake drains northward, the only one that does, since to north are the Alps and the rivers must go south to the Po valley.

The walker should consider the possibilities above Pella, near Madonna del Sasso, the name given to a small collection of villages and hamlets, an area which offers fine views of the lake. The church of the same name as the area is beautiful, both in construction and setting and contains some very interesting frescoes of the 18th century, and some fine earlier art-work: a 16th century painting and 17th century wooden crucifix.

Elsewhere, go to Orta S Giulio to see the lake's island. In the 4th century AD two brothers Giulio and Giuliano were sent from Rome to preach the gospel to the inhabitants of the wild area around the lake then known as Cusius. Giuliano founded his church at Gozzano and died there, but Giulio pressed on and reached the anvil-shaped headland opposite the lake's little island. The island attracted him immediately. It was gently wooded, quiet and remote and he wanted to be taken there to live as a hermit and teacher. The locals would not take him, telling him that it was inhabited by dragons and serpents, and was in the possession of the Powers of Darkness. Undeterred, Giulio flung his cloak on the water and stepped onto it. Then, to the

Ibex

astonishment of the locals, a wind picked up, blowing the cloak across the water, Giulio steering by using his staff as a rudder. By the time he reached the island the monsters had fled, over-awed by the sight of him and not daring to fight. Giulio landed and built his hermit's cell, where he lived for the rest of his life, converting and teaching the lake-dwellers. Today the island is jammed tight with buildings: there can be very few patches of soil that have not been, or are not, built upon.

Finally we move eastward from Lake Maggiore, reaching the green valleys north of Varese. Valcuvia is one of the greenest, most unspoilt valleys near any of the large lakes and though it is very short, only about 12 kilometres (7$^1/_2$ miles) long, it is worth the effort to visit. Valganna and Val Ceresio are also worth visiting, but our walk stays close to the modern city of Varese, visiting Campo dei Fiori, a famous beauty spot and viewpoint, reached by a walk up the Sacre Monte, an equally famous pilgrimage centre that winds up to the ridge of Campo.

Nath Vest Lake M.

Walk 1   Luino, Cannero and Cannobio

Map No:	KOMPASS Carta Turistica (1:50,000) Sheet 90 (Lago Maggiore/Lago di Varese)
Walking Time:	2 hours
Grade:	Easy
Highest Altitude:	Molineggi 454m (1,489 feet)
Lowest Altitude:	Cannobio 214m (702 feet)

This is a straight line walk, from Cannero to Cannobio necessitating a return by bus. A better idea altogether is to start from Luino on the opposite shore of the lake and to use the aliscafo, the hydrofoil, to make the connections, investing the walk with great theatre. Luino is the main centre on the eastern shore of Maggiore, and is famous as the preferred site for the birth of the great artist Bernardino Luini, though no absolute proof of this has yet been discovered. In the church of S Pietro in the eastern, up-hill, section of the town is an Adoration of the Magi widely attributed to the artist. In the main square of Luino, Piazza Garibaldi, is a statue of the leader of the Risorgimento, the first in Italy to be erected to him, and actually completed in his lifetime. When Garibaldi was defeated at the battle of Custozza he came here to try to raise an army to continue the war against the Austrians. Luino responded magnificently, giving Garibaldi great heart for the continuation of the struggle. The statue was erected to commemorate this event as much as the Great Man.

The hydrofoil ride across the lake shows off to perfection the northern, Swiss, end where the waters are framed by high, cloud-wisped peaks. The two fortified islands we pass are the Cannero Castles, one called il Sinasso, the other Castello Malpaga, though the latter name is frequently applied to the complex as a whole. The islands were home, in the 15th century, to five brothers who built the castles on them - the islands were joined by drawbridge, which must have been an elegant touch - and used them as a base to terrorise ships on the lake, which was then used as the main trading link in the area, roads being poor or non-existent, and to raid and rob the local villages. Eventually, in desperation, the local folk went to Milan and asked the Duke,

30

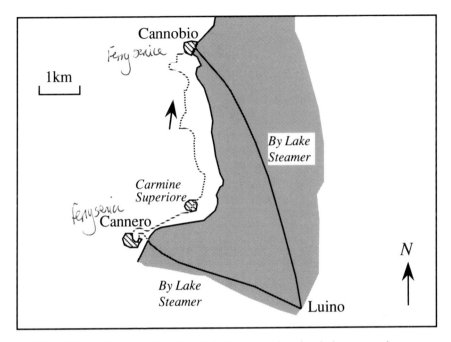

Filippo Maria Visconti, for help. He laid siege to the islands, but so good were the defences that it was two years before he defeated the pirates. The castles were slighted (partially destroyed) to prevent their re-use, though at a later time there was a brief, but unsuccessful, attempt to re-occupy the site. Today the islands are private, and visits are not allowed. Boat trips around them are possible however: ask at Cannero or Cannobio if you are interested.

Cannero was once described as a "Genoese Riviera in miniature...a pearl in a necklace of vineyards and villas". Such compliments long ago went to the heads of the town fathers, who added "Riviera" to the town's name. It is a pleasant spot - though the vineyards have largely gone - that will be heaving with people. You will be glad to have come by boat. Leave the town on the lakeside road for Cannobio - at the upper end of the town, that is, away from the lake - and, after about 400 metres, take the mule track that leads off left through a green landscape of gardens and cultivated farmland.

Follow the track to Carmine Superiore set on a characteristic rocky spur. This is a very old and very pretty village: look out for the ricetto, a rock cut hermitage from the earliest years of Christianity. The Romanesque church, consecrated to S Gottardo, is 14th century, as is its campanile and has some fine 15th century frescoes.

Leave Carmine along the mule track, ignoring the path to the right for

Carmine Superiore

Carmine Inferiore. The names here do not mean the better and the down-market villages, merely the upper and lower, relative to their positions above the lake. The track rises now, using big bends to gain height, and Molineggi is soon reached. Here there was, in ancient times, an important mill village and the remains of three or four mills can still be seen. From the old mills the track takes you gently down, with beautiful views over the lake, to Cannobio.

Cannobio is the first place of note on the Italian shore of Lake Maggiore for visitors arriving from Switzerland. It has a fine old quarter and a memorial stone to an attack by the townsfolk on an Austrian fleet moored offshore during the struggles of the Risorgimento. Near the town's harbour is a sanctuary church, Santuario della Pietà, where, in 1522, a picture of the Pietà - that is of the dead Christ attended by the Virgin Mary - began to shed real blood from Christ's wounds. This was a miracle of itself, but soon Cannobio was spared when Plague decimated the neighbourhood. Other miracles followed and Carlo Borromeo, of the local ruling family, Archbishop of Milan and later sanctified - see the walk starting near the Borromean Islands off Stresa - ordered a chapel to be built to enshrine the painting. The painting can still be seen, housed in an ornate silver frame, though it has never again shed real blood. Elsewhere, look for *il Pironi* a 15th century building in the shape of the bow of a ship, with a good loggia and elegant portico columns.

Walk 2 Stresa and the Mottarone

Map No:	KOMPASS Carta Turistica (1:50,000) Sheet 90 (Lago di Maggiore/Lago di Varese)
Walking Time:	4 hours
Grade:	Medium
Highest Altitude:	Monte Mottarone 1,491m (4,890 feet)
Lowest Altitude:	Stresa 200m (656 feet)

Stresa is, without doubt, the most elegant of all Lake Maggiore's towns, and probably the most famous of all the Italian lake resorts. The lakeside speaks of prosperity, with its walks through fine gardens, and its trees. On the other side of the lakeside road is an array of fine hotels, some of top international standard, and none more so than the "Grand Hotel et des Iles Borromées", a truly sumptuous building both inside and out. There is an old part to the town, and it is worth a visit. Piazza Cadorna is a little square filled with café seats where you can sit and sniff in the scent from the flowers that seem to grow everywhere.

When, in about 1630, Count Carlo III Borromeo first laid plans for the transformation of the island closest to Stresa, the island was flat and rocky, with a few fisherfolk houses and a chapel or two. What Count Carlo wanted was to change this island into his dream of a palatial ship anchored close to the shore. He started by shipping boatloads of soil to the island which his landscape architects used to create a ten-terraced garden, 40 metres (130 feet) high, sloping back from the island's southern tip to produce the effect of a snub-nosed boat. The result is an elaborate statement of the aims of Italian gardening, an architectural form in which man transforms nature into his own design, a sharp contrast to the English garden, where man aids nature in creating a naturalistic design. To the gardens Count Carlo and his sons - for the work outlived the designer, indeed the island was not finally completed until 1958, three centuries after Borromeo died - added a baroque palazzo, positively subdued externally in comparison to the gardens, but inside echoing the extravagance. The island was also transformed in name, Count

Carlo calling it Isola Isabella after his wife, the now familiar, shorter form flowing more gracefully from the tongue, and meaning "beautiful island".

The gardens are virtually indescribable, a rippling sensation of azaleas, rhododendrons, camellias, citrus trees and many more, with a collection of rarities, tea bushes, coffee trees, cork trees and others too numerous to mention. Everywhere there are beautiful staircases, too often flanked by fairly ordinary statuary to be sure, and through it all strut white peacocks, as flamboyant as their surroundings. The culmination of these terraces is the Unicorn Terrace with, as its crescendo, a shell-shaped construction of niches - some shell, some statue filled - statues, pinnacles and stairways overtopped by the unicorn symbol of the Borromeo family. Is it an over-ornate wedding cake in appalling taste, or a masterpiece of baroque composition?

The palazzo on the island has a wealth of rooms, some of great beauty, some of great lavishness, almost invariably lit by chandeliers of Murano glass.

The second of the trio of Borromean Islands is Isola Pescatori which, by contrast to Isola Bella, is almost drab. The island takes its name from the chief trade of the islanders, and on it the visitor can wander freely in narrow, sun-starved alleys, past drying fishing nets and visit the delightful, though much altered, 11th century church.

The third island, Isola Madre, is actually closer to Pallanza, from which is can also be reached, than it is to Stresa. Though the biggest of the three islands it is occupied by a single villa and its gardens - gardens which compete with those of Isola Bella on a botanical basis, though not at all in terms of lavishness. The gardens have been laid out to a plan, but it is best just to walk and admire, to become lost amid the plants and trees, the birds and the scents. There are orange and grapefruit, rhododendron and camellia, magnolia and azalea. And the visitor can try to spot the rarities, the Egyptian papyrus, the banana, tapioca and pineapple. The island's 18th century villa is simple, but charming and stands besides its own chapel where there are tombs of the Borromeo family. Inside it is again simple and elegant, a great contrast to the villa on Isola Bella.

One of the best views of the Borromean Islands is to be had from the top of the mountain that backs Stresa, a mountain usually called *il* - rather than *Monte* - Mottarone. From Carciano, close to Stresa a funivia goes up the mountain. There is also a toll road to the top. Why should anyone want to walk ? I think the only answer is that the journey is the satisfaction rather than the summit, and the walk allows an exploration of some very interesting sites on the way.

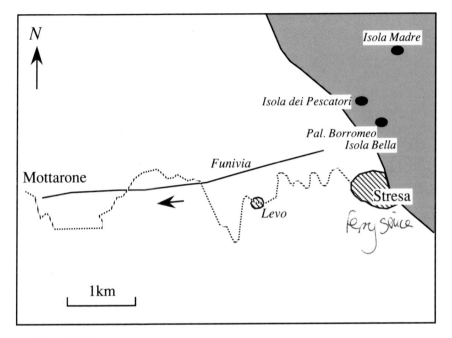

The Walk

From Stresa's Palazzo dei Congressi take the road west under the railway bridge and go right into a one way street. Bear right again on the road signed for Levo and Someraro. Go left into Via Selvalungo - signed for Levo - and follow the road to where Strada del Pioggio leads steeply off to the right. Here take the mule track to the left and follow it in to Levo, a fine hillside village.

Go to the south end of the village and take Via Fante Purissima, a cobbled street that leads steeply up to a chapel. Beyond, opposite No. 26, take the mule track that leads up to a road. Go right. Here is the entrance to the Alpine Gardens of Alpino, one of the finest gardens of its kind in Europe and a must for all gardeners. Go right to reach the intermediate station of the funivia. From here to the top the walk is not well marked and requires the use of a map.

Bear left before reaching the station, going up to buildings from where the alp is reached. Go steeply up the grass, staying close to the cable until a trackway is reached - after about 800 metres. Go left on the track to reach the Mottarone road at a sharp bend. From here the road is followed - but not on the tarmac. Go through the woodland to the side on a series of good to indifferent paths that frequently break out on the road. Finally a track is

Monte Rosa from the summit of the Mottarone

reached, to the right, for the Hotel Eden. Take this, going under the cableway, and go up the track from the hotel to the summit.

From the summit the view extends over the Alps from Monte Rosa to the Jungfrau, across the valleys around Domodossola and the lakes near Varese and over the Lombardy Plain to Milan. John Ruskin thought the Mottarone the "stupidest of mountains, grass all the way, no rocks, no interest, and the dullest view of the Alps". I could not disagree more.

Nr. Stresa.

Walk 3   Mergozzo and Monte Faiè

Map No:	KOMPASS Carta Turistica (1:50,000) Sheet 97 (Omegna - Varallo - Lago d'Orta)
Walking Time:	4 hours
Grade:	Easy
Highest Altitude:	Monte Faiè 1,352m (4,435 feet)
Lowest Altitude:	Mergozzo 204m (669 feet)

Where the Ossola valley, and the River Toce that flows down it, reaches Lake Maggiore the lake is incut to form a square bay. This square bay is rarely named, but the name Borromean is occasionally attached to it, for no better reason than within it, more or less, are the Borromean Islands of Isola Madre, Isola Pescatori and Isola Bella, all mentioned further in the introduction to Walk 2. The final miles that the Toce flows to reach the Borromean Bay is across a wide alluvial plain. But this plain is not straight, the river being pushed south by an intrusive mass of rock - Mont'Orfano. Mont'Orfano is a granitic mass left isolated by the glacier that once flowed slowly where the Toce flows quickly. In the village at the hill's foot, named Montorfano - a slightly confusing running-together of the hill's name - there are still a few marble cutters living in the houses of granite and marble, remnants of a former age when the stone in the Candoglia quarries was hand rather than machine cut.

North of this granite outlier ancient capture has created another lake, Lake Mergozzo, a pleasant stretch of water with fine camp sites on its eastern (Maggiore) edge. The village of the lake, one that also shares its name with the lake, is a fine place watched over by medieval towers and housing a good museum on the local history. There are two churches: the older, to S Maria, is 12th century marble Romanesque, while the much newer, 17th century, Assunta (Assumption) has a colonnade beside it with pilasters that remember when the village was struck by Plague in 1630. Our walk starts from there, but does not climb Mont'Orfano, going north instead to climb Monte Faiè, from where the views are much the same, except that they include Mont'Orfano.

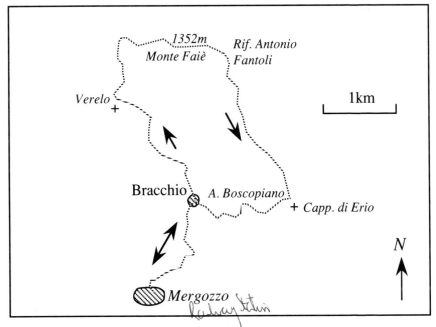

1352m
Monte Faiè

Rif. Antonio
Fantoli

Verelo
+

1km

Bracchio

A. Boscopiano

+ Capp. di Erio

N

Mergozzo *Railway station*

It is a moot point of course, but I would contend that the view to, rather than of, the solitary hill is better.

The Walk

From Mergozzo's railway station (on the line from Milan to Switzerland via the Simplon Tunnel) walk into the centre of the village. At the traffic lights go left towards Bracchio where the road ends. Go through the village, passing the church - a fine Romanesque church with an older (11th century) campanile - on the left, to reach the last houses. There bear left on a mule track to Verecio. From the hamlet take the path for Alpe Vercio and the Baita di Pianezza. The path goes steadily up hill offering the walker an unrivalled view over the cava (quarries) of Candoglia to the left. The stone from the quarries here was used to build the Duomo (cathedral) of Milan, as a stone on the summit of Monte Faiè, soon reached, notes.

The introduction to Walk 4 will mention the stone cutting, and the method of transportation from Candoglia to Milan - by river, lake, river and canal - but a few further facts are worth noting. One is that the Duomo was actually built by the citizens of Milan who gave up their time to labour on the construction site. A stone in the Duomo says that the building started in

1386, but a contemporary report notes that on 17 September 1387 a group of armourers started work on the foundations. Another interesting fact is that Milan had canals. The city had these dug in the early days of the City States and when completed they rivalled those of any city (except Venice of course). The Candoglia stone was delivered partially finished and inscribed *ad usum fabricae* (for building use) so that it could avoid city taxes. However, the years of free labour given to the church authorities and the occasional "accidental" re-routing of the stone to other projects which meant that work on the Duomo was delayed gave rise to the Milanese expression AUF, meaning working for nothing or being forced to take a long wait.

Candoglia marble is a superb building stone as it is both easily worked, free of defects and a delightful colour, being white with a pinkish tinge and blue-veined.

From the summit of Monte Faiè the view is impressive: to the west are the Alps of the Swiss border, while to the north are the high peaks of the Val d'Ossola side valleys. To the south are the lakes - Maggiore, Mergozzo and the hollow of Orta, peeping around the right flank of Mont'Orfano, the conical hill beyond Lake Mergozzo.

From the top go down the track signed for the Rifugio Fantoli (owned by the Pallanza group of the CAI and open daily in Summer, but only at weekends in Spring and Autumn), a fine track that threads its way through beech woods, with occasional glimpses across Lake Maggiore's Borromean Bay. From the Rifugio go down the lane to the chapel of Erfo (at 662 metres - 2,171 feet), the view ahead over the lakes and Val d'Ossola being a constant companion. From the chapel take the track for Alpe Boscopiano and continue to the village of Bracchio passed by the outward route. From the village reverse the outward route back to Mergozzo.

Walk 4 Cascata del Toce

Map No:	KOMPASS Carta Turistica (1:50,000) Sheet 89 (Domodossola)
Walking Time:	7 hours
Grade:	Difficult
Highest Altitude:	Rifugio 3A 2,980m (9,774 feet)
Lowest Altitude:	Sotto Frua 1,510m (4,953 feet)

One of the very best ways of crossing into Italy by road is over the Simplon Pass, the high-sided, tight Gondoschlucht - as the Swiss would call the gorge - being a delight, and the Val Divedro beyond the border being almost as good. Val Divedro leads to the Ossola valley, reaching it near Domodossola from where it is only a handful of miles to Lake Maggiore. Even those miles - it is actually about 20 or so for those assuming my handful is measured by finger counting and are wondering what sort of hands I possess - are interesting. Close to Lake Maggiore, but even closer to Lake Mergozzo a tiny lake that precedes it, look to the left as you approach Candoglia. The quarries in the hillside here were once owned by Milan's Visconti family and they gave stone from them to build the cathedral (Duomo) at Milan, the stone being shipped along Lake Maggiore, then by river and finally along Milan's ancient - but now largely disappeared - canal system.

Branching out from Val d'Ossola are a number of fine valleys. Val Anzasca leads almost to the foot of Monte Rosa and has the famous ski resort of Macugnaga at its head; Val Antrona is quieter, more secretive, a good place for the walker; Val Vegezzo leads to Locarno on the Swiss shore of Lake Maggiore by way of a number of interesting villages: and Val Formazza. The people living in this last valley are Walser rather than Italian, arriving here over the Gries Pass from the Valais in the 12th century. Val Formazza is famous for the Cascata del Toce, claimed to be the most beautiful waterfall in Europe. This walk visits that falls.

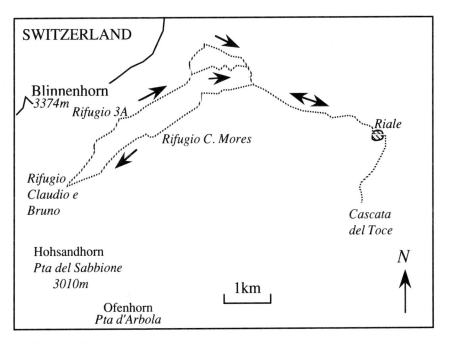

The Walk

The walk starts at Sotto Frua, a hamlet in the upper reaches of the Val Formazza, and close to the base of the famous falls. The falls are at their best on Sundays (!) when water that is diverted from them to drive a hydro-electric power station during the period Monday to Saturday is allowed to follow its normal course. If this sounds no way to treat a waterfall that could be a major tourist attraction, remember that there are many who have been to the Val Seriana (a valley running north from Bergamo) to see Europe's highest waterfall and have found it dry, all of its water piped off to the turbines. Before throwing up your hands in horror, it is worth remembering that Italy has no natural energy reserves - coal, oil, gas - of its own and an energy hungry economy. The Italians see the occasional use of water from such sources - the Cascata del Serio is "opened" on certain advertised dates during the year - as preferable to the currently available options.

Cascata del Toce is 143 metres (469 feet) high and 60 metres (197 feet) wide at its base. In form it is more of a slide than a fall, but that is no criticism, the Cascata is really very special.

Take the track on the right of the falls to reach Frue, a high plain popular with amateur geologists for its glacial erratics - boulders brought in from elsewhere by now melted Ice Age glaciers - where it joins a metalled road leading to Lake Morasco, at 1,815 metres (5,953 feet) and reachable by bus from Formazza if you wish to shorten the route. If continuing by foot, follow the River Toce, ignoring a path to the right for the Passo S Giacomo, and going through the village of Riale.

Follow the river back to the dam at the eastern end of Lake Morasco - all the local lakes are natural, but have been dammed to provide water for hydro-electric power generation. Go along the lake's northern shore to reach the ENEL (Italian Electricity) cableway. On the left side of the cableway towers is a steep path: take this to reach a wooden sign giving the direction of Route 9. Take this path, crossing the Toce and toiling up to Lake dei Babbioni and the Rifugio Mores (2,550 metres - 8,364 feet) from where there are magnificent views, none more so than that of the Sabbione Glacier falling into the lake from the high peaks to the west. These peaks represent the border between Switzerland and Italy and have dual names. To the south-west is the beautiful Punta dell'Arbola (Ofenhorn) with, from left to right, the Punta del Sabbione (Hohsandhorn), the Blinnenhorn - the exception to the rule, a peak known only by its German name, and the highest local top at 3,374 metres (11,067 feet) - the Corno Rosso (Rothorn) and, due north, the Punta dei Camosci (Bettelmatthorn). The last peak is named, in Italian, for the chamois which is often seen near here. The local country is a Zona Rifugio, an area closed to the hunter to protect the animals and birds. Other interesting animals that may be seen include marmots - which you are more likely to hear than see, their high-pitched alarm whistle frequently piercing the air, alpine hares and the stoat, each of which the very lucky visitor may see in winter white. Golden eagles are also seen working the thermals above the ridges.

Take Route 9B which goes down to the lake's dam, crosses it and goes above the north shore to Rifugio Claudio Bruno (2,750 metres - 9,020 feet) from where the Sabbione Glacier is seen in full glory. Take the track behind the Rifugio through an alp alive with colour in Spring, and then across rocky ground to reach Rifugio 3A (at 2,980 metres - 9,774 feet). Close by is the Siedel Glacier where summer skiing is possible, and a close up view of the high peaks of Blinnenhorn and Corno Rosso. The hut's curious name derives from the initials of Anna, Attilio and Alessendro, three young people who are leading lights in Operation Matto Grosso, part of the Mission for Latin America organisation which raises money for the underprivileged in South and Central America.

To return to Sotto Frua follow the glacier's edge to Rifugio Citte di Busto. Be cautious here: if there is a lot of snow on the ground away from the glacier do not attempt this route as you may finish up on the glacier itself, no happy

Cascata del Toce

Rifugio 3A

place for those without experience. If you are in any doubt, reverse the outward route as far as the Lake dei Sabbione dam and take the track to the Rifugio Citte di Busto by crossing the flat ground of Piano dei Camosci (are those goal-posts over there ?).

From the Rifugio there are two tracks, a direct descent to Lake Morasco and a longer, but much easier one going slightly north to the alps of Bettelmatt and following the Valle di Morasco down to the lake. Whichever route is taken, the outward route is followed from Lake Morasco back to the start.

Walk 5 Pino sul Lago Maggiore and Monte di Pino

Map No:	KOMPASS Carta Turistica (1:50,000) Sheet 90 (Lago Maggiore/Lago di Varese)
Walking Time:	6 hours
Grade:	Medium
Highest Altitude:	Monte di Pino 886m (2,906 feet)
Lowest Altitude	Pino sul Lago Maggiore 293m (961 feet)

Railway station   (time from Luino)

Pino sul Lago Maggiore has the longest name of any village in Italy.

It is a pleasant village with little more than 300 inhabitants, situated on a rocky promontory called the Sasso (stone) di Pino, and was once fortified, a tower from the Middle Ages now housing the town hall. By the Middle Ages though the site was already an old one, excavations in 1964 finding a Celtic tomb with two cinerary urns in copper, believed to date from the 5th century BC.

The Walk

From the railway station in the village take the road to Tronzano-Bassano, looking out for a mule track that runs parallel to the road to reach the village of Tronzano, with its fine views over the northern end of the lake. The village has a magnificent Romanesque campanile dating from the 11th or, perhaps, 12th century, attached to the church of S Maria. The Oratory of S Maria dei Disciplinati has a very fine fresco from the early 16th century attributed to the Lombard school of artists.

From the village continue on the mule track, soon reaching the church of S Maria Assunta, a well set church with another good Romanesque campanile in grey stone. From the church a narrow road leads quickly to the village of Bassano, a piled up village of great character.

A mule track leaves from the square of the village, heading for the Montagne di Bassano, the Bassano mountains, passing several recently renovated rifugios before reaching the dam at the northern end of Lake Delio. From here there are two tracks: that on the right goes up to the Passo Forcora,

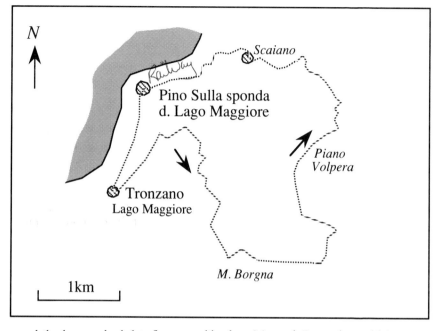

while that on the left is flatter, and leads to Monti di Pino where old farms once stood in the centre of cultivated ground. Today the farms have been deserted, the land is reverting to nature. If it were not for the renovation of some of the farms for weekend walkers the whole area would be in ruins.

Follow the track down through Val Molinera to reach a cross-roads. There follow the track signed for Monti di Caviano (Centocampi) which is actually across the border in Switzerland (Canton Ticino). Until 1960 almost all the farmhouses of Alpe, which is soon passed, had steep roofs made of straw that were extended to ground level. Sadly only a few sections of these exotic roofs can now be seen.

There is a curious legend about the origins of this little village. It is said that one day the devil offered the sexton of the village church 100 fields, a great prize, in exchange for his soul, the exchange to be made that night, between the services to be held at 6pm and 6am. The sexton accepted, but soon changed his mind and hid in the campanile hoping to protect himself. At dawn, when the devil had only one field left to prepare, the sexton began to ring the bells for the early morning service. The devil realised that he had been betrayed disappeared in a fury into a hole of the mountain. This story explains the name Centocampi, one hundred fields, that is often used for the area around Monti di Caviano.

Northern Lake Maggiore

From Centocampi continue down the broad, well-signed mule track to reach a fork. Take the signed path for Caviano, but branch off left for Scaiano, going through that hamlet and on down to Dirinella on the border between Italy and Switzerland. Go over the border, a passport will be needed, and along the lake shore to the bridge over the inflowing Molinera stream. Beyond is a road leading back to Pino.

Walk 6   Curiglia and Monteviasco

Map No:	KOMPASS Carta Turistica (1:50,000) Sheet 90 (Lago Maggiore/Lago di Varese)
Walking Time:	4 hours
Grade:	Easy
Highest Altitude:	Alpe Fontanelle 1,081m (3,546 feet)
Lowest Altitude:	Curiglia 670m (2,198 feet)

Sandwiched between the north-eastern shore of Lake Maggiore and the Swiss border is a lush, green land, its valleys thickly forested. It is a country where the villages are small and thinly scattered, a good area for the walker. The Italians, recognising this have waymarked the Via Verde Varesina, the Green Road of Varese (the local regional capital) through the best of the scenery. It visits Val Veddasca, one of the largest, and best, of the valleys stretching back from the lake to the Swiss border. Perched on the side of that valley is that most remarkable feature in modern Europe, a village not reached by roads. It is said to be a journey of a 1,000 steps to Monteviasco. Our walk will test this theory.

The Walk

A road leads from Luino to Dumenza, and from the latter village Curiglia is reached by a road that is often too narrow and twisty. The compensation is that it takes you through superb country. And it isn't very long before you reach Curiglia. Those wanting to avoid the drive will need to wait for a Sunday, as the bus from Luino to the village runs only on that day.

Park in Curiglia and take the road that goes to Ponte di Piero, the last point reached by road in Val Veddasca. From the bridge a mule track rises sharply to Monteviasco, about 500 feet above. The introduction said that the village was not reached by road. This is true, but does imply that the villagers have to walk this mule track twice daily. That was true until very recently, but is no longer true - today they can use a cable-car. So can you if you wish, cutting the climb down to a few minutes of idling.

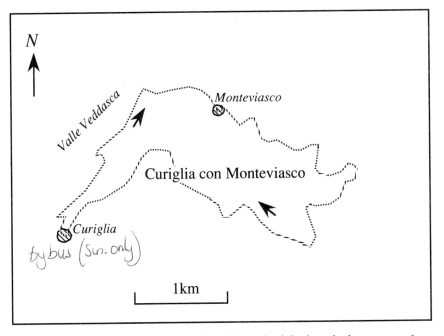

Monteviasco is a picturesque little village which had, at the beginning of the century, 380 inhabitants. Today the houses, for the most part restored, are mainly holiday homes, the permanent residents having fallen in number to about 20. The houses are all built with dry-stone walling, and each has a lobbie, a balcony. These were not built solely to take full advantage of the impressive views. They also have a practical value, being outside passages which link together the rooms of the house. The roofs are covered by piode, flat stone slabs cut to bed with each other. As with all the mountain houses, the windows are small to keep out winter's storms. Note too that fine door architraves, made in chestnut and occasionally carved with the date of construction.

The origins of Monteviasco are tied up with an old story. In the time of the Spanish domination of Lombardy, four deserters from the army of occupation took refuge in Val Veddasca, choosing this secret spot to build their houses. Soon the men's solitary life began to weary them, so they decided to kidnap some girls from the nearest village, Biegno, on the opposite side of the valley. They waited for a night when the Biegno menfolk were out on the mountain pastures, and raided the village, kidnapping four girls. News of the crime spread fast through the valley, and a small army of local men was assembled, armed with sticks, sickles and pitchforks. They marched on Monteviasco, where they found that girls were happy with their lot, and declined to return to Biegno.

From Monteviasco a mule-track heads off towards the Swiss border through Viaschina. The track gains a little height, but gradually, all the real climbing is over now, and reaches Alpe Polisa (at 1,050 metres - 3,444 feet) where there is a marked track for Alpe Corte and the Passo Agario. Ignore this, our track being virtually flat now and going through fine country to Alpe Fontanelle (at 1,081 metres - 3,546 feet, the high point of the route). Continue past the river - even in summer, if there has been a particularly snowy winter you can have snowslides here - to reach Alpe Cortetti where there are now-roofless alpine huts inside which the brambles grow. The huts were deserted after the 1939-45 War.

A hut once used by the local Forest Guard is passed, and then the track goes through a most beautiful beechwood to reach Alpe di Viasco. Curiglia is only a short step away now down a well-trodden path.

The village is superbly set, and inhabited by orcks (owls) so-called because those who worked out of the village, always came back the same day, even if it meant going through the dense woodland when it was completely dark. About 300 metres from the village, beside the road, is the 14th century Sanctuary Church of Tronchedo. The name is Spanish for tree-trunk, and is said to derive from another incident during the Spanish domination. There was a landslide, and the inhabitants were only able to reach the valley by placing a large tree trunk over a gully across which one person could pass at a time. A man who had been away from the village for some days and did not know about the landslide and the trunk came home at night, riding across the tree without ever realising it was there. In the morning everybody was astonished, not least the man himself, and to celebrate what was seen as a miraculous delivery from death the villagers built a small chapel dedicated to the Madonna di Tronchedo, Our Lady of the Tree Trunk.

Walk 7   Monte Ceneri Pass, Monte Tamaro, Monte Lema, Dumenza and Luino

Map No:	KOMPASS Carta Turistica (1:50,000) Sheet 90 (Lago Maggiore/Lago di Varese)
Walking Time:	7 hours
Grade:	Medium
Highest Altitude:	Monte Tamaro 1,961m (6,432 feet)
Lowest Altitude:	Dumenza 440m (1,443 feet)

This is a superb route, staying high for most of its length, and connecting the high peaks of the Sottoceneri, in the Swiss canton of Ticino, with the high peaks of the ridge that forms the border between Switzerland and Italy. The route then descends to Lake Maggiore. As it therefore starts in one country and finishes in the other passports are required.

From Luino, on Lake Maggiore's eastern shore, take the train towards Bellinzona, changing trains at Giubiasco for one bound for Lugano. Get off at Rivera, where the walk starts.

Note that the initial part of the walk makes use of a cableway, reducing considerably the amount of climbing required on the route.

The Walk

Walk to the base of the cableway that rises to Alpe Foppa (at 1,350 metres - 4,428 feet). There is a plan to extend the cableway up to Motto Rotondo, about 600 metres (2,000 feet) higher. When that happens the impact on the walk time will be significant as it will reduce the climbing involved to trivial amounts - although there will still be the long descent to Lake Maggiore. For the moment, from the top station at Alpe Foppa take the path north-east along the rocky rib of Motto Rotondo to the reach the Rifugio Monte Tamaro (at 1,928 metres - 6,324 feet), from where Monte Tamaro is easily climbed by a rocky path. The view from the summit is spectacular, taking in much of Swiss Ticino as well as Lake Maggiore and the high alps around Monte Rosa.

From the summit follow the signs for Bassa di Indemini (the low point in

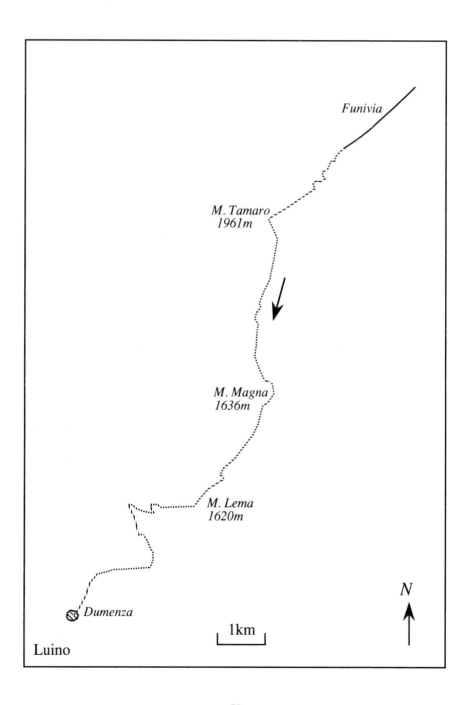

Funivia

M. Tamaro
1961m

M. Magna
1636m

M. Lema
1620m

Dumenza

Luino

1km

N

On the ridge from Monte Tamaro to Monte Lema

The summit cross, Monte Lema

this section of the walk, at 1,723 metres - 5,651 feet) continuing Bassa di Montoia, from where the track traverses, but does not climb, Monte Gradiccioli, and then climbs Monte Pola (1,741 metres - 5,710 feet). Descend to the Passo Agario (1,574 metres - 5,163 feet) from where a short cut leads down to Monteviasco (see Walk 6).

From the pass the track climbs and descends all the way to Rifugio Lema set almost on top of Monte Lema and set astride the Swiss-Italian border. The path in this section of the walk is frequently rocky, and occasionally cut out of the rock, but is nowhere dangerous and can be followed by any experienced fell walker. Those who wish to follow the walk over a weekend can stay at the Rifugio, awaking to, and having breakfast in front of, one of the great views of the lake area.

The summit of Monte Lema can be reached in a few minutes for a slightly extended view over Lakes Lugano and Maggiore and the Swiss-Italian Alps. Leave from the summit along a signed track taking to Rifugio Alpe Predecolo (1,184 metres - 3,884 feet) which is wholly in Italian territory. From the Rifugio the path continues to Alpe Pra Bernardo and on to Pra Fontana (1,162 metres - 3,811 feet). From Pra Fontana a steep track goes down into the Val del Cortesel to reach Trezzino (at only 470 metres - 1,542 feet - to give some measure of the speed of descent). Within the village is the Sanctuary of Trezzo, with a walkway bordered by Chapels of the Via Crucis. Once there was a convent here, a place of pilgrimage and every year, in the middle of August, there is a festival to commemorate the pilgrimages.

Trezzino is little more than a suburb of Dumenza, a village dedicated to the memory of the Madonna della Freccia, Our Lady of the Arrow, a dedication that remembers the legend that the villagers were once threatened by a dragon, but were saved when it was killed by an archer. From Dumenza a bus runs down the last few miles to Luino.

Walk 8   Laveno to Calde via Sasso del Ferro

Map No:	KOMPASS Carta Turistica (1:50,000) Sheet 90 (Lago Maggiore/Lago di Varese)
Walking Time:	5 hours
Grade:	Medium
Highest Altitude:	Monte Teggia 1,103m (3,618 feet)
Lowest Altitude:	Laveno 207m (679 feet)

Laveno, at the foot of Monte Sasso del Ferro, is famous for its ceramic work, the history of the local industry being shown in the museum of the Terraglia di Cerro, at the Palazzo Perabo, in the nearby village of Cerro del Lago Maggiore. The tradition is now continued by the sculptor Sergio Tapia Radic who has a studio at 177 Via Labiena - the Varese road out of the town. This Cuban-born artist produces superb, modern ceramic work among his range, though his chief work is religious, in bronze or plaster.

Close to Cerro, just a few miles south, is the church of Santa Caterina del Sasso, one of the most famous sites on the whole of the lake. The story goes that a local, Alberto Bessozi, thief, usurer and all-round rogue, was out on the lake one day when a sudden squall over-turned his boat leaving him in great danger of drowning. Alberto prayed hard, promising that if he survived the ordeal he would change his ways. A wave threw him up on to a ledge below a sheer cliff, and there he stayed for the rest of his life, giving away all his money and goods and building a small hermitage church on the ledge. Alberto survived by hauling food up from passing boats, his winch still remaining at the site. After he died he was buried within a rock crevice, but years later his body was re-discovered, miraculously free from decay and this too can still be seen at the site, a surprising sight in its sacred vestments lying within a glass case. The church is much enlarged from Alberto's time, though his heritage is incorporated in the new building, and even the fabric has seen miraculous events. Some years ago a huge rock fell through the roof and would have destroyed the whole building had it not come to rest supported on three bricks in a fashion that appeared to defy both engineering logic and the laws of gravity. Only recently has the church finally been re-opened.

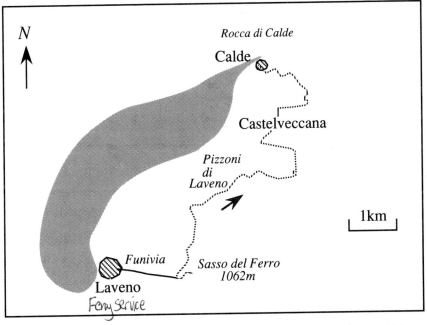

Note that though the data given above implies an ascent of some 900 metres (3,000 feet) this is not the case, all of the climbing being accomplished as a passenger on Laveno's remarkable cableway.

The Walk

Our route starts by going through Laveno to the funivia (cableway) at the base of the Sasso del Ferro. The cableway is one of the great adventures of Lake Maggiore, passengers standing in two-person buckets that finish at waist level so that there is no interruption to the view - both out over the town and lake, or down to the ground. The exposure is not that great, no more than ordinarily terrifying, and does allow a very good view of the butterflies that congregate along the corridor cleared through the woodland beneath the buckets.

The top station is at Poggio S Elsa (at 950 metres - 3,116 feet) a panoramic viewpoint, the view including Monte Rosa and the Vallesane Alps. From the top station a steep track leads up to the summit of the Sasso del Ferro (at 1,062 metres - 3,483 feet), though this trip is optional, our route taking a downhill track towards Casere from where a narrow road is followed to Cuvignone. From that village a track is followed to Passo Barbe where another road is

Laveno and Sasso del Ferro from the lake

reached and followed along the fine ridge of Pizzoni which goes over Monte Teggia and down to Passo del Cuvignone. The views on this section of the walk are exquisite, dominated by that across the lake which is seen to perfection from here.

The track continues in straightforward and fine style, dropping down to the Rifugio De Grana-Adamoli, and continuing to descend as it rounds the hillside above the lake to reach the village of Pira. Take the track south out of the village which leads to Calde, a small tourist resort lying beneath the Rocca di Calde, a natural fortress reinforced by walls, banks and ditches in the 10th century, but destroyed in the 15th century when it was recognised as too useful for those wishing to control the lake.

From Calde buses run frequently to take the walker the few miles back to Laveno.

Walk 9   Sacre Monte di Varese and Campo dei Fiori

Map No:	KOMPASS Carta Turistica (1:50,000) Sheet 90 (Lago Maggiore/Lago di Varese)
Walking Time:	8 hours
Grade:	Medium
Highest Altitude:	Vetta Paradiso 1,227m (4,025 feet)
Lowest Altitude	Orino 442m (1,450 feet)

Varese is a modern city set between the city of Como and the eastern shore of Lake Maggiore. Close to it are several smaller lakes, one of which, named for the town, is important archaeologically, finds from Neolithic and Bronze Age lake dwellers having been found on Isolino Virginia, a small island near its western shore. North of Varese there are fine wooded valleys, one of which holds Arcumeggia, a village in which the outer walls of the houses have been frescoed by leading Italian artists so that the village is a living, open-air gallery of contemporary Italian art

Our walk here does not visit Arcumeggia or, indeed, one of the valleys, taking the ridge of Campo dei Fiori, a famous panoramic ridge. Close to the ridge's eastern end is the Sacre Monte. In the early 15th century the church of Santa Maria at the top of the hill here was the repository of a wooden Madonna history attributed to the hand of St Luke himself, making the church a place of pilgrimage. In the 17th and 18th centuries a Via Sacra was laid out up the hill to the church, the Way having decorated 14 chapels set along it. General opinion suggests that the 7th chapel, with frescoes by Morazzone, is the better decorated.

At the top of the Way the church of S Maria del Monte still holds the wooden Madonna - called the Black Madonna because of the colour of the (natural) wood. In the village around the church there are two museums, one to the work of the artist Ludovico Poglaghi who was responsible for the huge central doors of Milan's Duomo (cathedral), while the other is of the art collection of Baron Baroffio. On top of the Campo dei Fiori is a study centre that includes an observatory and alpine flower collection, both of which can be visited.

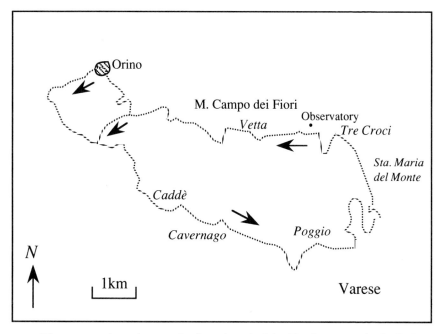

There is ample parking at the first chapel of the Via Sacra, reached off of the Varese to Brinzio road.

The Walk

From the first chapel of Sacre Monte pass under the arch near the statue of the Madonna and follow the Via Sacra past the 14 chapels built in the 17th and 18th centuries. Near the beginning of the way there is a fountain and two others are passed later near the two arches that divide the "Mysteries". At the end of the way, which is about 2 kilometres ($1^1/_4$ miles) long, is the large Moses Fountain, close to which is the hill-top village of S Maria del Monte with its museums.

Go to the right of the fountain on a road that passes beneath the Convent of Romite Sisters to reach a large square. From this take a wide track that passes under the old cableway to Campo dei Fiori and reaches a road beside which is a track going up to the top of Monte Pizzella. At a fork go left across a wide piece of alp (pasture) into a pine wood. Soon you will reach the old cableway top station. From here go left on the road near the entrance to the old Grand Hotel, a sadly decaying masterpiece of Art Nouveau. Close by is Grotta Marelli, an interesting show cave.

Go up the steps to the church and take the Via delle Gloria, a wide track beside which are reminders of past glories of the Italian Army. Ahead now is the summit of Monte Tre Croci (1,111 metres - 3,644 feet) from where the view is superb in all directions. Go north on a track recently prepared by the army to reach the Battery, a piazzale with another fine view to which, this time, is added the rock climbing training ground of the Varese group of the CAI (Italian Alpine Club).

Take the military road which goes down to the left pass the guest house of Pensione Irma to reach woodland. Follow the signs - still yellow splashes and Route 1 - to another piazzale with seats. Here there is a gate into the Centro Geofisico del Campo dei Fiori, the observatory and botanical study centre.

From the square follow the Via Verde Varesine a new footpath signed by the Province of Varese. At Sign 5 there is a fork: the path to the right here goes to the top of Vetta Paradiso, at 1,227 metres (4,025 feet) the highest point on the Campo dei Fiori from where there is a good view of Monte Rosa across Lake Maggiore. Continue along the Via Verde to reach Sign 15 where a small iron cross remembers the death of a hang-glider pilot near the spot. Campo dei Fiori was one of the first places in Italy where hang-gliders were used, the man commemorated here having been killed before the science of the machines' flight was well understood.

Bends in the path now take the walker to another piazzale named for the old Orina fort that stood just to the south. Again the square offers good views of the wooded Varesian valleys. Continue to a bend where a sign points out Route 2 on the right. Take this down through woodland to the village of Orina. The way through the wood is less clear than the route to this point: go down for 800 metres to a fork where there is an arrow on a tree to the left - to the left here is a short cut through Pra Camare that reaches the main route about 600 metres further on. Go left on the main route (signed for Route 10). To follow the complete walk take the right fork and follow the Route 2 signs diligently to reach a road. Go left past an old fountain inscribed "1882". Go through chestnut and fir tree woods, going over the Valle di Mezzo on a bridge to reach the first houses (in Via Gorizia) of Orino. The plaque on this route commemorates three soldiers killed by a bomb in 1922.

To the right in the village is the main square and church, while to the left are the football field and the seedling nursery of the Corpo Forestale (a Forestry Commission of sorts). Take the track signed for Route 10 (in a yellow square) and follow it to the point where the short cut from Pra Camare joins. Bear right along the undulating path to a farm, Fienile delle Pianezze. The track descends here, but soon levels out. Ignore a track to the right for Gavirate and then another, also on the right, for Comerio. The track

A pilgrim on the Sacre Monte

continues on level ground passing several farms, and then crosses the streams of two small valleys - Valle Frentina and Valle delle Tacca - on wooden bridges to reach Cavernago where it is joined by another track coming from Comerio to the south.

Continue on the main track, going east across the shallow valleys of Valle del Cappone and Valle delle Barassina to reach a farm (Zambella). Beyond the farm 10 minutes of walking, some of it in a pleasant, small wood, brings you to a metalled road. Go left on this for 300 metres to where it ends. There go right on a path between two fenced enclosures. Soon you bear right on to a lane that becomes a road near the gate of a big park. Follow the road to the Pian delle Croce - the villa here was once the Villa Pirelli - and bear left on a track to another road. Go left to reach Via Piatti in the village of Velate.

Go left into Via Duca d'Aosta, passing the church. Take Via Adda out of the village - there is a good view of Sacre Monte from here - and bear right on a road, following red arrows and splashes (Route 9). Route 9 bears right off the road into Val Vellone, going right to cross the stream and going up through the wood on the far side. The track is much bigger now, and leads past the old bus terminal (for Sacre Monte) and an old cableway station to reach a piazzale. From the square steps lead up to the first chapel.

Lake Lugano and Lake Como

Lake Lugano is a fox-shaped piece of water - nose at Ponte Tresa, ear at Agno, paws at Porto Ceresio and Capolago, and a huge tail all the way to Porlezza. From nose to tail the lake is 36 kilometres (22$^1/_2$ miles) long. It is always narrow, the maximum width - not measured into one of the many bays - being only about 2 kilometres (1$^1/_4$ miles) just south of the bridge at Melide.

The greater part of the lake's shoreline lies in Switzerland, the city of Lugano being the largest city in the Swiss canton of Ticino, though once it was under the influence of Milan, having been caught up in the wars between Como and Milan in the early middle ages. The Swiss took the city and the neighbouring country from Milan in 1512, and have held it over since, the land freed from Austrian rule in the Risorgimento being the entire claim by the new Italian state, which never made any serious attempt to annexe Italian-speaking Swiss territories.

Italy holds the north-western shoreline, and the eastern tip of the lake - and thus the deepest water, the lake reaching down 288 metres (945 feet) off the village of Albogasio - together with the enclosure of Campione. The town of Campione d'Italia is entirely surrounded by Switzerland, earning foreign currency by operating a very successful casino.

At its eastern end Lake Lugano is hemmed in by high hills, the hills split by fine valleys. Val Rezzo climbs up through vineyards to meadows, beech woods and rocks. At Buggiolo a side road leads to Seghebbia a convenient starting point for walks along the ridge from Cime di Fiorina to Monte Garzirola that forms the border between Italy and Switzerland.

Beyond Buggiolo the road rises further and then drops down into Val Cavargna, a beautiful, rugged, heavily wooded, valley - certainly the best in this area near the Swiss border. Cavargna is the seat of the Museo della Valle, the Museum of Val Cavargna, opened only very recently and still expanding. From Cavargna the ride down the valley is a winding one, but one where each turn brings new scenic delights. There are several villages in the valley: S. Nazzaro Val Cavargna with the best of the views; S. Bartolomeo Val Cavargna, the biggest village with a rebuilt church that still contains some fine medieval art work; and Cusino, where the campanile seems to be held up by faith alone.

Finally, in the upper reaches of Val Sanagra there is also good walking.

On the opposite side of the lake, the southern side, is Val d'Intelvi, a fine, airy series of valleys with many delightful villages. At the other end of the valley is Lake Como.

Though Lake Como is only the third biggest of these northern Lakes, with an area of 148 square kilometres (55 square miles), it has the longest perimeter, a shore line of over 170 kilometres (106 miles). The glacier that cut out its hollow, the Adda glacier, divided around the promontory ridge south of Bellagio, forming two arms. These arms, extending to the towns of Como and Lecco, give the lake an inverted Y-shape, and explain the lengthy perimeter. Como has another claim, that of being Europe's deepest lake. The deepest part lies between Argegno and Nesso, reaching 410 metres (1345 feet). Yet another claim is that of most names to describe a single stretch of water. The arm of the upturned Y that extends towards Lecco is known locally as Lake Lecco, and this arm feeds the River Adda which is the whole lake's only outflow. North of Bellagio the upright of the Y is known as Lake Colico, and the whole lake is also called Lario. The latter derives from Lacus Larionus, the Roman name for the lake, the Romans having taken control of the area in the second century BC.

The lake is the most enclosed of the major lakes, its northern reaches showing to perfection the V-cut hollow of its glacial birth. This enclosed nature seems to give Lake Como its own atmosphere: a pureness of air and a pureness of colour that combine to produce an almost magical quality. This has long been noted by artists, many of whom have visited and fallen in love with the lake. Goethe, Flaubert, Robert Browning, Tennyson, Liszt and Tschaikovsky to name but a very few. Shelley said that "the beauty of this lake surpasses everything I have seen hitherto" and Liszt even went as far as to name his Como-born daughter, who would grow up to become Wagner's wife, after the lake.

Como has the best of the shore's from a point of view of the walker, with fine high ridges offering tremendous views over the lake, those ridges on the western shore also allow Lake Lugano to be seen. At the northern end there is Berlinghera, a superb upland area of wooded valleys famous for their wildlife, while the triangle of upland between the lower arms of the lake is almost as good. The eastern shore is best of all, the peaks of the Grigne and Resegone being almost Dolomitic in their rugged sharpness. Here, of all the areas close to the lakes, the walker is really at home.

Walk 10   Monte Generoso

Map No:	KOMPASS Carta Turistica (1:50,000) Sheet 91 (Lago di Como/Lago di Lugano)
Walking Time:	1 hour
Grade:	Easy
Highest Altitude:	Monte Generoso 1,701m (5,579 feet)
Lowest Altitude	Breggia 1,300m (4,264 feet)

This walk has several important plusses. Monte Generoso offer a superb panorama with, in the right conditions, most of the Lombardy Plain visible, and the Apennines rising as its back edge. More locally, the view extends over the Valle d'Intelvi, one of the best valleys running into one of the big lakes, and Lake Lugano. Another bonus is that the walk starts and ends in Switzerland, but spends most of its time in Italy, crossing the border on the way out and on the way back. Remember to carry your passport: for most of the time the border guards are as scrupulous on this high peak as they are on the autostrada crossing points.

Monte Generoso itself is climbed the easy way, by railway. The little train is 100 years old and leaves from the town of Capolago on the Swiss shore of Lake Lugano, at the extreme southern end of the lake - and close to the cross-border autostrada. In about half an hour the visitor arrives at the top to be greeted not only by the terminal station and a view, but by an hotel with a bar and self-service restaurant and a solarium for more than 600 people. In addition there is a little chapel dedicated to the Madonna, to the side of which is a stairway to the actual top.

The hotel is a good place to stay overnight, offering typically Swiss meals and dancing on Saturdays from June to September. Watching the sun rise from the top is one of the (the only?) great free shows of Switzerland, and the flowers on the great alps below the summit are spectacular. It is mainly for the flowers and shrubs that this walk and the following one have been included. To get the best out of them it is better to come in Spring or early Summer, though even late Summer trips are worthwhile.

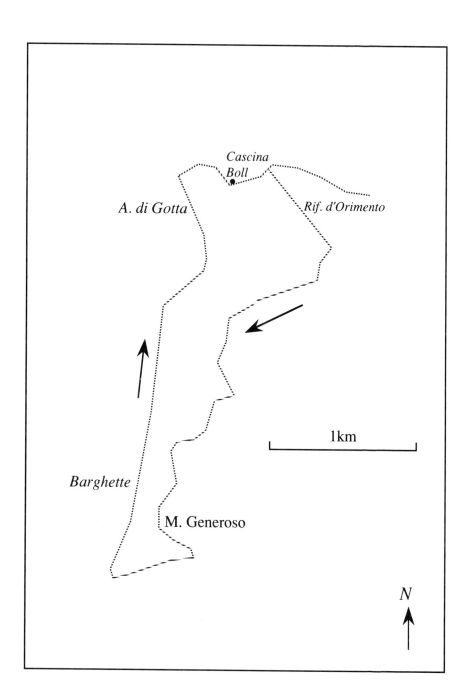

The Walk

From the restaurant at the right of the little chapel, take the track that passes below the summit of Monte Generoso and the rocky towers of Baraghetto. In spring the whole area here is covered by primula auricula. In English we would call this Auricula Cowslip, as it looks like a giant cowslip, but with the centre of each flower white rather than yellow, but the Italian name, *Orecchia d'Orso*, is more poetic. It means the ear of the bear.

The final top of the summit ridge is Piancaccia. From it follow the path north-east, with spectacularly panoramic views, the path bordered by shrubby green alder. Do not stray too far right down the slope of the Pescio Alp. The path soon passes a bolla, a trough-like rainwater catcher used by the alp farm animals. The path runs along the edge of the wooded Alpi di Gotta, beyond which it bears eastward towards the farmhouse of Cascina di Boll, travelling across pasture covered, in summer, with yellow laburnum and purple willow gentian.

From the farm house the view is excellent, extending across Lake Lugano to the Denti della Vecchia (the old woman's teeth), to the north, with the peaks of the Valsolda to the right and the more distant Engadine Alps. Take the track eastward - noticing the point where a path comes in from the right - to Alpe d'Orimento, a little group of houses and farm huddled around a tiny church. In summer there is a restaurant here, a pleasant place to spend the hotter part of the day. From the village it is a short distance only to Pizzo Croce, where there are trenches built as defences during the First World War, a war which never came this way. From Pizzo Croce you can see, in the distance, Monte Disgrazia (3,678 m), Monte Legnone (2,610 m) and peaks of the Grigne with, in front, the Bisbino (1,325 m), the Galbiga (1,697 m), and Sasso di Gordone (1,409 m).

To return to Generoso, retrace your steps back towards Cascina di Boll, forking left on the path noticed on the outward journey. The new path, across the Breggia Alp, meanders through the low green alder, with a studding of sycamore trees. The occasional crude shelters you pass are baitocch, temporary bivouacs built by hunters at the start of each hunting season. The green alder and sycamore is replaced by cherries and maple, with yellow oxlip and the deep violet, but poisonous, monkshood, as we reach the now-deserted buildings of the Pescio, once home to nine families and over 500 animals.

Ahead now is the Swiss border, the final part of the walk back to the railway being along the border itself. I hope you remembered your passport....

Monte Generoso from Chiasso

Lanzo d'Intelvi

Walk 11   Monte Generoso to the Intelvi Valley

Map No:	KOMPASS Carta Turistica (1:50,000) Sheet 91 (Lago di Como/Lago di Lugano)
Walking Time:	2 hours
Grade:	Easy
Highest Altitude:	Monte Generoso 1,701m (5,579 feet)
Lowest Altitude:	Lanzo d'Intelvi 892m (2,926 feet)

This second walk from Monte Generoso is, like the first, a walk for flower lovers, being especially good in Spring and early Summer. The advantages of Monte Generoso as a start point have been fully explored in the previous walk. This walk has the extra advantage of exploring the Valle d'Intelvi, a very fine valley, though it must be stressed that unless the route is completed as an out and back route then some of the exploration is enforced, return to the start point - Capolago on southern Lake Lugano - being by bus to Como, and then by train across the border.

As with Walk 10, the route crosses the Italian-Swiss border: do not forget your passport.

The Walk

Follow Walk 10 to Alpe d'Orimento and continue along the asphalted road to Rifugio del Criste, once an army barracks but now owned by the regional (Como) office of the CAI, the Italian Alpine Club. Continue along the road for 200 metres and then take the old road with its superb views of the Grigna and the Grignetta. This is open country, with an alpine flora, but the road soon enters a wood of fir trees. This lasts for about 300 metres before open country is reached again, this time above the excellent Alpe Nuova. From here the view includes the Gradiccioli, the Denti delle Vecchia and Valsolda.

Ahead now there is a choice. To the left is a path across Alpe Nuova, in summer a pasture, in winter one of the ski slopes (a piano) of Lanzo. Beyond the Alpe the route follows the stream in the Val Caprera - look for the waymarker arrows painted on the stones sticking out of the water.

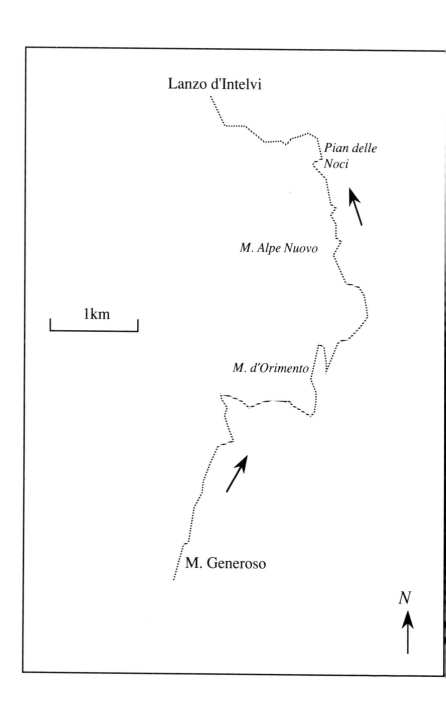

The second possibility, the better route, goes to the right towards the "Zoca da l'Alp Nova", a little valley covered by junipers and ferns. In spring, after winter's snow has dissolved away the area is carpeted with white crocus.

After the alternative routes join the way is straightforward to Dosso Brione, a geologically interesting area for its glacial erratics - rocks brought to the area by ice movements. Here too there is evidence of the importance of winter sports to the area, though the skilift tends to be used by children rather than adults. Continue to the road at Piano delle Noci, named for the walnut trees that once grew in profusion here, but are now much rarer. The reason for the loss is the use by the local folk of walnut oil to light their lamps before electricity reached this far end of the Intelvi Valley. Follow the road into Lanzo.

The Intelvi Valley, of which Lanzo is the most important village, is not one, but a series of fine, airy valleys many of the villages of which have churches by the Maestri Comacini. These were a brotherhood of medieval architects and sculptors who rejected personal fame in favour of collective brilliance. As a result none of the group are known by name. You would imagine that such behaviour would be unique, but there was another group of architects who did the same thing. These were based in Campione, a town on the shore of Lake Lugano that is Italian but completely surrounded by Switzerland. Campione makes the most of its isolation, running a casino for the benefit, in the main, of the Swiss.

Intelvi has a fine history, Neolithic and Roman remains having been discovered here, and those interested in that history should visit the museum of the valley in Scaria, a small village to the east of Lanzo.

Lanzo itself is a sporting town, with golf, tennis, horse-riding and skiing. It is also close to two of Italy's most famous viewpoints. The first, to the south-west at Sighignola, is known as the Balcony of Italy, while the second, at Belvedere to the north-east is equally good. From the latter viewpoint Monte Rosa, the Matterhorn and the Jungfrau are visible, as is Campo dei Fiori outside Varese.

Walk 12   From Cavargna to Val Solda

Map No:	KOMPASS Carta Turistica (1:50,000) Sheet 91 (Lago di Como/Lago di Lugano)
Walking Time:	5 hours
Grade:	Medium
Highest Altitude:	Monti Calone 1,400m (4,600 feet)
Lowest Altitude:	Dasio di Valsolda 580m (1,902 feet)

This route is of special interest to those who are staying in Porlezza, a pretty town on the Italian shore of Lake Lugano. The town's name derives from Portius Retiae, its Roman name, given at a time when it was the gateway to the land of Retiae, a people who lived in the hilly country beyond. In the Middle Ages the town was a favourite with artists, all of them attracted by its lakeside/mountain position and its clear air. One who came was Giugliemo della Porta, whose position in the history of art does not reflect the fact that he was the favourite pupil of Michelangelo.

The walk starts at Cavargna and ends at Dasio, a village in Valsolda, each of which is connected by bus to Porlezza allowing a circular trip to be completed with the minimum of fuss. The walk is actually the majority of the third (of four) parts of the Walk of Four Valleys, the best known and most popular of the linked pathways of Como. I say linked pathways because there is no equivalent here of an official long-distance footpath.

The Four Valleys Walk starts at Breglia, close to Menaggio on the shore of Lake Como - and starting point of Walk 15 - and crosses the valleys of Val Sanagra, Val Cavargna, Val Rezzo and Val Solda. The walker following the route here sets foot in three of those four, as well as climbing to a high pass where he can stand with one foot in Switzerland and the other in Italy. The walk is waymarked throughout with a paint bar comprising red, white and red bands - usually on an aluminium plate - and with the number 3 and, occasionally, the name, Sentiero delle 4 Valli, prominently displayed.

Note that Cavargna, a pleasant village where our walk starts, is set at 1,071 metres (3,513 feet), so that the amount of climbing involved is not to be judged from the figures given in the box above. Those figures refer to the total

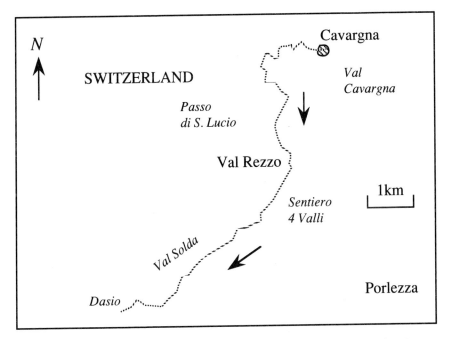

descent, over 800 metres, the route involving much less, approximately 350 metres, of ascent.

The Walk

Cavargna, our starting village, is picturesque and beautifully set. Its church is only 20 years old despite the 17th century campanile and is decorated with contemporary art. The Museo della Valle, a museum specialising in the history and folk-lore of the Val Cavargna is small, but worth some time. It items on ancient crafts includes the chimney sweep, and the cross-border smuggler.

Leave Cavargna from close to the church, in the upper part of the village, the path soon reaching a steep slope on which stands the old barracks of the Guardia di Finanza, now holiday house of the municipality. It is a moot point whether the smugglers in the museum or the Revenue men remembered here are getting the largest helping of respect. The path now enters a beautiful beech wood called the Bosco Sacro, the "holy wood" because it protects the village from avalanches. Beyond is the narrow Val Marda.

Cross the valley's stream over the excellent new bridge built in iron and wood recently to reach a twisting track pass farms that takes you to the open

Porlezza

pastures of Monti Calone, at about 1,400 metres (4,600 feet). From here it is possible to reach the church of S. Lucio, a 14th century, but recently restored, building set right on the Swiss border, at Passo S Lucio - involving a 140 metre (460 foot) climb, allow 30 minutes - or Monte Garzirola, at 2,116 metres (6,940 feet), allow 2 hours, where you can stay overnight in another former border police barracks now transformed into a Rifugio

From Calone take the new track down through beautiful woodland to Roccoli near the watershed between Val Cavargna and Val Rezzo. Turn down the road that connects Buggiolo to Passo S. Lucio when it is reached, going as far as the fountain near the little chapel of Madonna del Cepp, where there is a picnic area. Leave the road on the right and go through a beautiful beech wood - look out for the waymarks on the trees - to reach farms set near a river. The path becomes a descending mule track which you leave, left, at a fork to reach the village of Seghebbia. Here it is possible to eat and to stay overnight.

South from the village the path crosses pastures with fine views and a delightful river (the Torrente Rezzo draining the Val Rezzo) to reach, beyond another excellent wood, an old Rifugio called Pramarzio, once a resting place for smugglers. Ahead now the path follows a short, but delightful, transverse valley that links Val Rezzo with Val Riccola in which the hamlet of Pralungo

Val Cavargna

occupies a good, very green, site. The path drops gently, passing through yet more fine woodland to Alpe Riccola where the scenery is Dolomite-like with limestone outcrops, colourful plant-life and a lot of water.

The resemblance increases as the Passo Stretto - the last, and tightest, pass before the Valsolda - is reached. A mule track goes through the pass, descending beyond it to bring the walker his first view of Lake Lugano. The next building is not an ex-border police site, but one belonging to the local forestry commission, so if you are looking for a rest it is best to continue on the rapidly descending track to Ranco, one of the very best local camp sites. Ahead now is the final 30 minute section of the walk, the mule track going steeply down to the end of the Valsolda valley, and crossing the Solda river to reach the village of Dasio di Valsolda.

The village of Dasio is a good centre for visiting the inhabited section of the Valsolda. It is a good valley, rich in artist interest and scenic treasure. At Castello, at the lowest end of the valley, there is a museum to the local history and art, while nearby Oria was the home of Antonio Fogazzaro, one of the most famous of Italian authors, but a man little known in the English speaking world.

Walk 13 Cernobbio and Argegno

Map No:	KOMPASS Carta Turistica (1:50,000) Sheet 91 (Lago di Como/Lago di Lugano)
Walking Time:	6 hours
Grade:	Medium
Highest Altitude:	Rifugio Prabello 1,200m (3,936 feet)
Lowest Altitude:	Cernobbio 201m (659 feet)

Cernobbio, the first town on Lake Como's western shore, and close to Como city, is a pretty place, most famous for the Villa d'Este. Despite its name the villa was built in the 16th century for Cardinal Gallio, Secretary of State to Pope Gregory XIII and a man rich beyond the dreams of most who actively sought wealth rather than the, apparently, more austere life of the cleric. What the Cardinal built is what we see, with some minor alterations required by its new use as a hotel. In the 18th century the villa was owned by the local Austrian commander-in-chief and later was occupied by Caroline of Brunswick, wife of the British Prince of Wales, George Frederick, later George IV. If rumour is to be believed, and it certainly was at the time, Caroline spent most of her time at the villa in leisure and pleasure, her pleasures being chiefly of, shall we say, an adult nature. The scandal was great locally, and eventually found its way back to London, forming the basis of her now notorious trial. The British enjoyed a rhyme at her expense when she returned to Westminster for the trial -

> "Most Gracious queen, we thee implore
> To go away and sin no more;
> Or if that effort be too great,
> To go away at any rate."

The rhyme contains an inaccuracy - because Caroline was not crowned, or even present, when George was crowned, another scandal, and its chanting was eventually dropped when the country decided they did not like the new king one bit and so, since Caroline did not get on with him either, took his wife to their hearts.

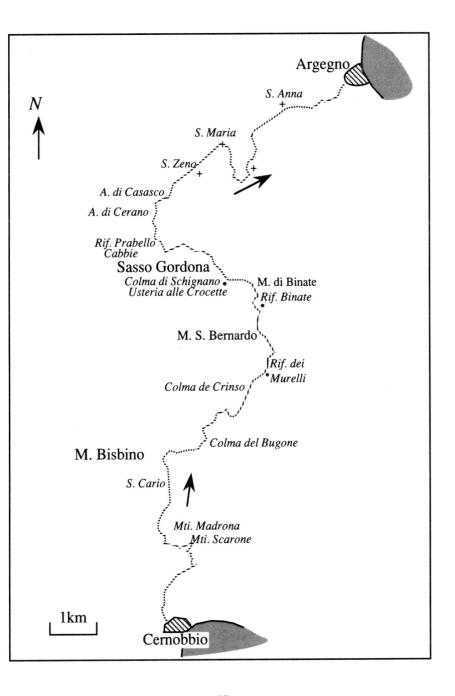

N

Argegno

S. Anna

S. Maria

S. Zeno

A. di Casasco

A. di Cerano

Rif. Prabello
Cabbie

Sasso Gordona

Colma di Schignano
Usteria alle Crocette

M. di Binate

Rif. Binate

M. S. Bernardo

Rif. dei
Murelli

Colma de Crinso

Colma del Bugone

M. Bisbino

S. Cario

Mti. Madrona
Mti. Scarone

1km

Cernobbio

But by this time Caroline had left Villa d'Este for good leaving behind the fading scent of scandal and the name, for the Queen believed herself to be descended from the Este family.

Today the Villa is an hotel, certainly the grandest for many miles and with a claim to being the grandest on any of the Italian Lakes. With its beautiful gardens and an interior that is a treasure house of art, it would seem to be the absolute height of luxury, with just a slight qualm about whether it would be possible to shake off the feeling that you were sleeping in a museum. The hotel boasts a swimming pool that floats on the lake (!) and - on the other side of the road - a folly fortress.

Our long, but straightforward walk has many potential refreshment stops, the majority of them being converted military buildings dating from the 1914-18 War.

The Walk

From Piazza Mazzini (Mazzini Square) in Cernobbio take the road for Monte Bisbino for about 500 metres and then go left to Stimianico and follow the pedestrian way, passing in front of Casnedo church to reach the square in front of the church in Rovenna. From the square the Alta Via, marked by red/white/red splashes runs parallel to the road up Monti Scarone. The land here is deliberately uncultivated (lying fallow) at the time of writing. Go through a chestnut wood and rejoin the road for Monti Madrona (at 850 metres - 2,788 feet) topped by a group of well-set alpine huts. Continue on the road until the first zig-zag bend, and there take the track ahead which climbs up past the chapel of S Carlo chapel and, beyond, reaches the road for Monte Bisbino. Do not go left towards the summit, but cross the road and follow the track opposite to a fork. There take the right branch to reach Ca' Bossi, a theological college.

Bear left on the lane, going down slightly and passing behind an old building to reach Colma del Bugone, a private Rifugio at 1,119 metres (3,670 feet) from where the view of the lake is exquisite. Continue on the Alta Via, going through fine fir tree woodland and ignoring side tracks to reach another Rifugio, the Colma del Crinco. From this hut the track stays on the ridge top and is practically flat all the way to Rifugio dei Muselli, owned by the Moltrasio group of the CAI (Italian Alpine Club).

Take the road from the Rifugio all the way to Mortirolo and there bear right to reach Monti di Binate and the Rifugio Binate (at 1,200 metres - 3,936 feet - and owned by the Cantu group of the CAI). Northward now the Alta Via passes through cultivated farmland and some alp pasture to reach the

Colma di Schignano, occasionally known as the Osteria delle Crocette, a private Rifugio, but one that is open for the sale of very welcome coffee.

To the west is Sasso Gordona, a peak on the Swiss-Italian border. The Alta Via follows an old military road around the foot of the peak on the side of a valley that is a side valley of the Val d'Intelvi. At the Colina di Prabello the track reaches the Rifugio Prabello (of the Monte Olimpino CAI).

As a worthwhile variation to the main route, the top of Sasso Gordona (1,410 metres - 4,625 feet) can be reached in about 30 minutes by a track that leads up through fine pasture. The route passes trenches built during the 1914-18 War, a grim reminder of old hatreds, but in May is colourful with peonies. From the summit of Sasso Gordona the view across the Val d'Intelvi is superb, as is that into Switzerland's Valle di Muggio.

Those not taking the variant route do not take the road for Casasco, a pretty Val d'Intevi village, reached at the Rifugio Prabello, but cross it and continue along the Alta Via that goes steeply down across alp pasture and through woods to reach the alpine hut of Alpe di Cerano (at 960 metres - 3,149 feet) set on the watershed between Valle d'Intelvi and Val Breggia.

Beyond the Rifugio a short road section leads to the road from Casasco to Erbonne. Erbonne, to the left, is the last village in Italy, set under Monte Generoso. The village womenfolk still wash clothes in the big, outdoor communal washing "pool" beneath a substantial roof, but open to the cutting wind that must make the job a misery on all but summer's more luxurious days. From the village all walks are into Switzerland, the border marked by nothing more than a line on a map. But we go right to reach Alpe di Cerano from where the old military road leads down to Alpe di Casasco, and on into the shallow Val Bisurco.

Cross the valley's stream right at the foot of Monte San Zeno, the peak that defines Val Bisurco's eastern end, and go steeply down the winding track to reach the little church of S Maria set at the outskirts of the village of Ovrascio di Schignano (at 607 metres - 1,991 feet), a village well-known for its annual carnival (ask at the tourist office in Argegno for details of when it will be taking place). Take the road through the village and on to the hamlet of Occagno. There, take the mule track on the left down to the church - about 200 metres - and go right, past it, on a track that follows the River Telo, then bears right away from the river to reach the main road close to the old church of S Anna. From the church the mule track runs parallel to the road, reaching Argegno close to the Roman bridge over the River Telo. This approach to the town shows it at its best, an array of half-round tiled houses poking up through the tree canopies. If you have the time, explore the bustling town, or take the funivia up to Pigra from where the view of the lake is excellent, no less

Cernobbio and Monte Bisbino

extensive than those from the latter stages of our route, but with a less cluttered foreground.

From Argegno the return to Cernobbio is very easy, and takes considerably less time than our walk. Buses or the lake steamer reaches the start village in about 20 minutes.

Walk 14   Ossuccio to San Benedetto in Val Parlana

Map No:	KOMPASS Carta Turistica (1:50,000) Sheet 91 (Lago di Como/Lago di Lugano)
Walking Time:	3 hours
Grade:	Easy
Highest Altitude:	San Benedetto 815m (2,673 feet)
Lowest Altitude:	Valmadrera 250m (820 feet)

This fine walk uses both sides of Val Perlana a fine valley reaching back into the hills from the western shore of Lake Como. At the valley's mouth is Ossuccio a village close to two of Como's most famous landmarks. Off shore is Isola Comacina, now a green, empty island - in fact Lake Como's only island - but one that in the 12th century held one of the richest cities on the lake. The city was known as Crisopoli, the City of Gold - often, but wrongly, written as Christopoli, the City of Christ - and it challenged the city of Como for domination of the lake. The challenge involved siding with Milan in the Ten Years War, but this was, ultimately, the wrong side. Como asked for help from Barbarossa and he brought an army to destroy Milan. Como sent its army to the island and the city there was razed to the ground. So great was the destruction that no one ever attempted to resurrect the city. Today on the Saturday following St John's Day the destruction is commemorated by a firework display on the lake, followed on the Sunday by a Mass in the (few) remains of the island city's basilica.

On shore and close to the island is the campanile of Ospedaletto probably the most photographed tower on - and now adopted as the symbol of - the lake, and rightly so, its slender, elegant form being a real show-stopper.

The Walk

From the village of Ossuccio take the road towards Preda and the sanctuary chapel of Santa Maria del Soccorso. Literally the dedication is to the Virgin of Assistance, though the word is now more frequently used in a medical sense, Pronto Soccorso meaning First Aid. The road can be driven to a higher

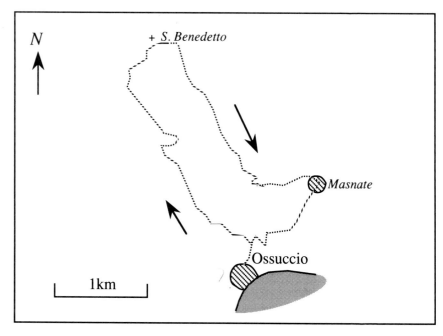

parking area close to the start of a Via Sacre with 14 little chapels in Baroque style with the Mysteries of the Rosary represented by life-size plaster figures. The chapels were built between 1635 and 1710 and are considered to be masterpieces of the Intelvese School.

The sanctuary chapel itself is at the end of the Via Sacra, and is set on the Orrido del Tufo, 221 metres (725 feet) above lake level. Orrido means horrible, but is frequently applied to a gorge, the more so if it is narrow, tight and dark. The chapel is 16th century, though it was enlarged in the 18th. Inside there is a fine old painting of the Virgin with Sant'Eufemia and other Saints and a marble Madonna and Child.

From the square by the sanctuary take the steep little lane to the Baite di Preda, bearing right when a mule track goes left towards the Rifugio Boffalora. Our route, Route No. 35, goes up the side of the Val Perlana, a fine valley going through the small hamlets of Garubio and Pelenden with its group of alpine huts, built in the 11th century as the property of the monks of San Benedetto, but now in ruins.

The path crosses the Val Perlana's stream, the Torrente San Benedetto, continuing through good country to reach the Basilica of San Benedetto, built in the 11th century in Romanesque style. It is generally agreed that the church is the best preserved of all Como's churches from that era. Near the

The campanile, Ospedaletto

campanile are the remains of the old Cluniac monastery that once stood here. Of the monastery, which did service as farm buildings after it ceased to house monks, only a section of the cloisters remains.

Cross the valley's stream again close to the old site, and head towards the lake on the paved mule track that follows the left side of the valley: you are now on Route 36. Follow the mule track to the farm buildings of Pianes, which is passed on the left side. Beyond, the route is delightful, the track meandering through soft country, with occasional steep descents, to reach Abbadia dell'Acquafredda. There was a church on the site here from the early 16th century, but it needs an expert eye to discern it among the massive rebuilding that took place between 1680 and 1784. Of the present abbey it can be truly said that it is imposing.

Equally grand is the view of the lake from Abbadia, the waters of the central section being seen between cypresses. Directly below is the snout of Punta di Lavedo, also known as Balbianello Point after the Villa Balbianello on its tip. This fine villa can only be reached from the lake, the landing stage being famous for the statue of St Francis who welcomes visitors, and for the elegance of its architecture. There are those who claim that the landing stage is the only place on the lake that can compete with Ospedaletto's campanile for the title of most photographed spot.

From the abbey take the road for Lenno for 200 metres, then go right crossing the Val Perlane stream for the final time on a track that reaches the chapels of the outward route. Return to Ossuccio, where you could end the walk by eating in one of the local trattorias. This part of the lake was once known as the *Zocca de l'Oli*, the oil bottle, for the number of olive trees and the quality of their oil. There is still an oil-mill in Ospedaletto and it will be local oil that flavours the lake fish and vegetables of your meal.

Walk 15   Breglia and Monte Grona

Map No:	KOMPASS Carta Turistica (1:50,000) Sheet 91 (Lago di Como/Lago di Lugano)
Walking Time:	4 hours
Grade:	Difficult
Highest Altitude:	Monte Grona 1,736m (5,694 feet)
Lowest Altitude	Breglia 749m (2,457 feet)

This walk starts from just beyond the hamlet of Breglia, a hamlet that is actually more of a "suburb" of the village of Plesio. To reach Plesio, go up the western shore of Lake Como to Menaggio and take the Lugano road out of that town. After a short, but twisty, distance look for the turning on the right for Loveno. Take this road, going through Loveno and on up another twisty road to Plesio and Breglia at its far edge. This road passes the bottling factory for "Chiarella" water, the local mineral water. If you are in your own car you can stop here and sample the water at the fountain the factory owners have thoughtfully set up on the front lawn. In case you are tempted, the sign here tells you that you are not allowed to bring your own containers for filling!

An alternative way of reaching the start is to take the lake steamer from Como city to Menaggio and the bus through to Breglia. Menaggio is the last town of fine villas on the western shore, the villages becoming increasingly workman-like the further north you go from here. Being a "frontier" town - it lies on the shortest route to Lugano and Switzerland - the town has a fair range of shops and facilities, rather more in fact than many of the more "holiday-centre" villages to the south. Loveno, through which we also pass, is an equally fine place to spend time, with its walled streets and interesting corners.

The Walk

This walk is waymarked throughout by red paint markers, and follows Route Nos 27 and 28.

Those who have driven to Breglia can drive the first few yards of the walk,

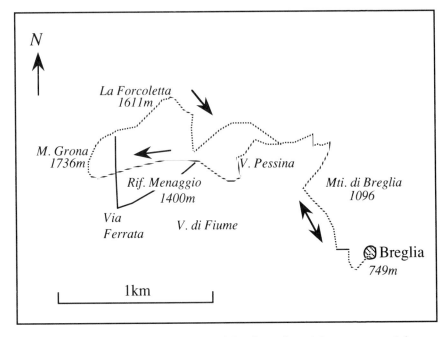

N

La Forcoletta
1611m

M. Grona
1736m

Rif. Menaggio
1400m

V. Pessina

Mti. di Breglia
1096

Via
Ferrata

V. di Fiume

Breglia
749m

1km

which takes the metalled road signed for the Rifugio Menaggio out of the hamlet. This road soon ends, the end being signalled by the cars all parked - in somewhat haphazard, but space efficient way - close to the start of the path to the Rifugio.

The pathway is actually a mule track, and rises through excellent woodland to reach a path to the left. Watch for this as it can be missed by the unwary even though it is well signed. Soon you will reach a small house with a prominent fountain. Here the path forks: take the left fork, the right one is the return route.

The path to the left turns south and goes through a deep and narrow valley and then ascends the far valley side to reach, and pass, a TV repeater station. Rifugio Menaggio is soon reached now, a welcome sight with an animal drinking trough that supplies cool water for drinking and pouring over a heated head. The Rifugio is open daily in summer, but only at weekends in the cooler months of spring and autumn.

Settle on the balcony with a glass of something and admire the view of the central and upper parts of Lake Como and the picturesque lump of the Grigne. Lake Como is at its best in these areas. To the south it is pretty rather than beautiful, but all that changes here. To the north the deep V-notch betrays its glacial origins, while below us the division into the Como and

Lecco arms around the point that holds Bellagio, the Pearl of the Lake, is almost beyond description. The point itself is Punta Spartivento, the point that divides the winds, an elegant as well as accurate description.

The view is improved with every step now, the path from the Rifugio being appropriately called the Via Panoramico, an Italian phrase that needs absolutely no translation. Via Panoramico is a variant (Variante A, the main path) of Route 28. Another variant, Variante D, follows the Via Ferrata del Centenario CAO, an iron way - see Walk 21A for a full explanation - to the top of Monte Grona, a route created to celebrate the centenary of the Como Alpine Club. The Via Ferrata follows the obvious candles of rock up the front of the peak, and on good days the walker is treated to a view of ant-like climbers on the route. Watch, perhaps next time you could return to try the route for yourself.

Via Panoramico begins behind the Rifugio - the route to the Via Ferrata goes across the front of the hut, but the routes will converge later - going through a narrow gully beyond which the view expands to include Lake Lugano. The route traverses the face of Monte Grona - look out for the climbers here - going in spectacular style between the rock towers to reach a steep grassy section of path. Be cautious here, this grass is shiny and can be treacherous for the unwary: if your boots are not suitable consider turning back as a slip could have serious consequences.

The route is more serious now the higher you go, culminating in a final tower of rock that requires the assistance of an in-situ wire rope.

Monte Grona is one of the best viewpoints around Lake Como, and is also interesting geologically, being the final dolomitic peak that separates the southern pre-Alps from the real (Lepontine) Alps.

The descent from the summit is also down a rope, though not the same one used for the ascent. Go in the opposite direction, reaching La Forcolleta (1,611 metres) from where the red and yellow paint marks of a variant of Route 28 lead comfortably back to Rifugio Menaggio. To return to Breglia the outward route can be reversed, or the slightly more difficult Sentiero Alto, can be followed. This goes north from the hut and is a little longer and certainly offers better views. However, in all but the early morning and early evening the route can be unbearably hot for the British walker. The track reaches the fork passed on the outward route. Now reverse the route to the mule track and back to Breglia.

Walk 16   The Alpine Huts of Berlinghera

Map No:	KOMPASS Carta Turistica (1:50,000) Sheet 92 (Chiavenna/Val Bregaglia)
Walking Time:	5 hours
Grade:	Easy
Highest Altitude:	Alpe Gigiai 1,630m (5,346 feet)
Lowest Altitude:	Montalto 1,030m (3,378 feet)

At the northern end of Lake Como the inflowing rivers of Mera and Adda - the former flowing in from the small Lake Mezzola, the latter from the Valtellina - define a triangular, low lying semi-marsh, the Piano di Spagna (literally the Spanish Plain), which is an important site for migrating birds. Close by, north of Como's extreme tip, is a lush land famous for its butter and cheese, and for woods that abound in berries and fungi, one of the local delicacies, as well as being home to many animals. Our route visits this area, taking a high valley close to Sasso Canale and Monte Berlinghera, on the flanks of which the pine woods are famous as the war-time refuge of the Partisans.

The Walk

On the north-western shore of Lake Como are the towns of Gravedona, Dongo and Sorico which, in the Middle Ages, formed an independent republic known as the Tre Pieve, which raised an army and fought against Federico Barbarossa when he attempted to annexe northern Italy. It was at Dongo that the fleeing Mussolini was captured by the Partisans in 1945, though it was at Azzano to the south that he was executed.

Take the west shore road past Dongo and Gravedona, but before reaching the final third of the Tre Pieve, just before Gera Lario - a popular centre for windsurfing - turn off for Montemezzo. This road winds up to Burano, and on to Montalto, with a charming church to S Lorenzo. Leave the car here.

Continue along the road - following signs for the Alta Vie dei Monte Lariani, the High Route of the Mountains of Lario, Lario being the Roman

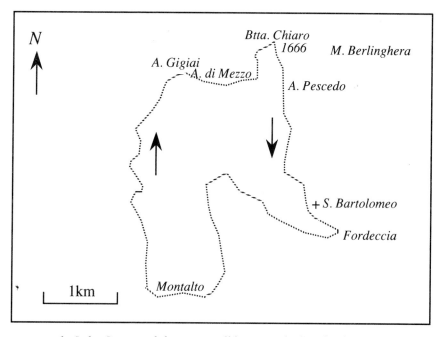

name for Lake Como and the name still being applied to the district - until it ends and there take the mule track that zig-zags up the hill to the north. This track offer fine views back across the river each time you pause for photography or a rest. Follow the track to the recently restored alpine hut of Alpe Gigiai (at 1,630 metres - 5,346 feet) from where there are fine views of the high peaks of Monte Berlinghera, to the east, and Sasso Canale, to the north-west. Continue east on level and gently falling ground, passing a terminone, a long wall that divides the pasture, and going through a wood to reach the Alpe di Mezzo where the alpine huts look like little villas. In the wood through which you have just walked, and indeed in all the woods on this route, be quiet and cautious and you may well see a cervi, as the Italians call the red deer.

Pass the huts of Alpe di Mezzo to reach the Bocchetta di Chiaro, the low point on the ridge that extends from Monte Berlinghera to the Sasso Canale. The pass here is an important site for migrating birds which use it as a short cut from the Mera valley to Lake Como. It is also noticeable for the signs pointing out the tracks of the Alte Via del Lario which uses the pass to link Sasso Canale with S Bartolomeo. Here too is an electricity power line pylon and, away from it, good views to Chiavenna and the mountains of the Bregaglia.

Bocchetta di Chiaro and Sasso Canale

Follow the Alta Via down to Alpe Pescado, close to Alpe di Mezzo, and by the pylon there go left on a track, signed with the yellow and red splashes of the High Route, through a delightful wood of Scots Pine, seemingly at home here despite the distance from the glens, that reaches S Bartolomeo (at 1,200 metres - 3,936 feet, and with a good little church). Follow the road through the village to reach the alp (pasture) of Fordeccia and a fine view of Lake Mezzola and the Piano di Spagna. Fordeccia is occasionally used as a launch point by hang-gliders.

Near the guest house there is a sign for the Alta Via that we again follow, going south through Piazza Lunga and down into the Valle di Sorico. The track goes around the head of the valley, crossing two streams and then going through a final section of (excellent) woodland to reach the road close to Montalto. Go right, back to your car.

On your return journey to Lake Como call in at the church in Montemezzo to see the frescoes of the Luini school and of Fiammenghino, an artist from about 1600 who committed a murder in Milan and hid away in the mountains here earning a living by church painting.

Walk 17 Como - Brunate - Lemna

Map No:	KOMPASS Carta Turistica (1:50,000) Sheet 91 (Lago di Como/Lago di Lugano)
Walking Time:	5 hours
Grade:	Medium
Highest Altitude:	Bocchetta di Lemna 1,167m (3,828 feet)
Lowest Altitude	Como 201m (659 feet)

This fine route is at its best in early spring when the slopes of Monte Bolletto and Monte Palanzone are alive with narcissus. Como, the start point, is the best city on any of the big lakes, a wonderful place full of airy squares, old and tight alleys, churches and monuments, and all set right on the lake which laps gently at the edge of Piazza Cavour at the heart of the city. Before starting the walk you must visit the cathedral (Duomo) and the Piazza San Fedele. The tower on the hill above the town is all that remains of the Baradello Castle built by Barbarossa in the mid-12th century. A century after its completion the castle became a prison as well as a fortress. The Torriani family, local lords, were defeated in battle by the Viscontis of Milan at the Battle of Desio in 1227. Ottone Visconti, who coupled the duties of general in the family army with those of Archbishop of Milan, imprisoned Napo Torriani and his family at the castle. Napo was not held inside, but in a metal cage that was suspended on the outside walls of the building. There, exposed to rain, snow, sun and wind he suffered for 18 months until he died, so it is said, when after going insane he beat his head against the bars of the cage. It is doubtful whether Napo ever enjoyed the glorious view of Lake Como from the castle walls.

The Walk

The walk starts from Como, but the first two hours of the five hour journey can be eliminated in fine style by taking the funivia to Brunate and the bus from there to the CAO's Capanna Rifugio just beyond S Maurizio.

In Como go to the Porta Vittoria, a superb 40 metre (130 foot) tower that

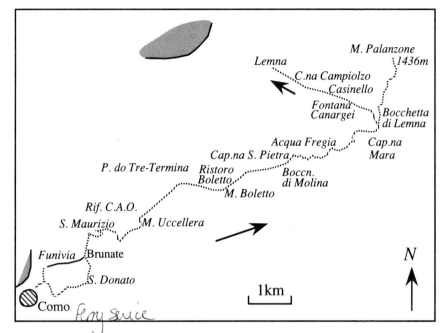

M. Palanzone
1436m
Lemna
C.na Campiolzo
Casinello
Fontana
Canargei
Bocchetta
di Lemna
Acqua Fregia
Cap.na S. Pietra
Cap.na
Mara
P. do Tre-Termina
Ristoro
Boletto
Boccn.
di Molina
M. Boletto
Rif. C.A.O.
S. Maurizio
M. Uccellera
Funivia
Brunate
S. Donato
Como
1km
N

is the best remaining part of the 12th century town walls - and through which
Garibaldi marched after liberating the city at the nearby battle of S Fermo
during the Risorgimento. Beyond is Via Cesare Battisti: go left along it and
along Via Tomaso beyond. At the end take the track between the houses into
a wood. Go through the hamlet of S Donato and, ignoring a turning, right,
to Garzolo, continue to Brunate. The walk takes about 40 minutes, the
funivia about 5 minutes, to reach another spot known, occasionally, as the
Balcony of the Alps.

Follow the road between villas and gardens to S Maurizio. Here there is a
29 metre (95 foot) tower built to celebrate the centenary of the death of
Alessandro Volta, a Como man. In Como itself there is a museum to the work
of the great physicist. Also at S Maurizio there is the first of many beautiful
panoramas of the Lake Como.

From San Maurizio continue along the road to the CAO Rifugio (all the
rifugios on this route are open daily in summer, but only at weekends in
winter) beside which there is a small church erected to the memory of the
alpini, mountain soldiers who died in the two Wars. Follow the road beside
the rifugio, somewhat unnecessarily waymarked in red and white into the
wood that shrouds the northern flank of Monte Ucelleria following it past
Baite Carle. Ignore the track to the left signed for Pertugio and that on the

right, a mule track, to Civiglio. When you reach the old Hotel Espena take the Vie Bel Paese to reach the Baite Boudelle and, beyond, the Baite Boletto. From the latter we traverse across the wooded summit of Monte Boletto descending the shallow peak's eastern flank to reach the Bocchetta di Moline and S Pietro Capanna (mountain hut).

From S Pietro follow the waymarked track (Route 5) across the north side of Monte Bolettone. The track crosses the very attractive Pian di Fo, passing the Acqua Fregia, a now dry spring. Ahead is the Bocchetta di Lemna, about 3 walking hours from Como, or less than 2 hours if the funivia and bus are used. From the Bocchetta a track leads to the forest road coming from the Val Bova and going to M. Palanzone, following new signs, this is Route 1 to Bellagio.

To reach the Rifugio of Capanna Mara go right, the hut being only about 5 minutes away. To continue to Lemna go left on the mule track signed in red and white for Route 4. The mule track takes the right side of the valley of Val di Gaggia, passing close to the pool of the now-dry spring of Fontana Canargei and going through superb woodland which offers tantalising glimpses of Lake Como. The mule track passes farms and the small hamlet of Bicogno, leading directly to the main square of Lemna, with its town hall, church and the restaurant where you have to buy your ticket for the return bus ride to Como about 13 kilometres (8 miles) away.

Those with an extra hour can complete the classic Vie delle Cime, reaching the top of Monte Palanzone (1,436 metres - 4,710 feet), from the Bocchetta di Lemna. Close to the summit is the Rifugio Palanzone, about 160 metres (525 feet) from the top, close to which is a cool spring and a gated cave. From the summit of Monte Palanzone the view extends to Monte Rosa, the Grigne and the Corni di Canzo. From the summit Route 6, also signed in red and white, descends to Palanzo where there is an interesting wine press dating from 1572. Buses run from Palanzo to Como.

Walk 18   Monte San Primo

Map No:	KOMPASS Carta Turistica (1:50,000) Sheet 91 (Lago di Como/Lago di Lugano)
Walking Time:	3 hours
Grade:	Easy
Highest Altitude:	Monte San Primo 1,686m (5,530 feet)
Lowest Altitude:	Parco Monte San Primo 1,107m (3,631 feet)

North of Bellagio, at Ghisallo, is a hill known to cyclists throughout the world and on its summit is a monument dedicated to the world's cyclists and a chapel erected for them. From the monument - which shows a cyclist with arm raised in triumph, or salute, or both - there is a superb view over the Lecco arm of Lake Como, with its backdrop of the Grigna mountains.

Close to the monument is Magreglio, one of the most romantic villages of the Valassina, the valley that cuts the High Brianza, the triangle of land spreading back from Bellagio and formed by the inverted-Y arms of Lake Como. From Magreglio a road runs across the high, flat Piano Rancio through which flows the River Lambro, called Menaresta in the local dialect, a word that means "intermittent", the river occasionally diving below ground level. At the end of the road is Parco Monte San Primo a very pleasant spot set in a valley at the foot of Monte San Primo. There are many second homes here, restaurants, an hotel and ski lifts, this being a popular, if small, resort. Our route starts in the square by the ski lifts.

The Walk

Go back to the road, and go along it to the gate that closes it to cars. Continue on the gravel road, a road that offers a tour of the upper Val Perlo in order to reach Alpe delle Ville, at 1,121 metres (3,677 feet). Go left here, on the track signed for the Rifugio Martina, a track which passes through the pasture of delightfully named Alpe of the Picet, the alp of robins. From the Rifugio there is an expansive view, especially good being that over Isola Comacina and Val

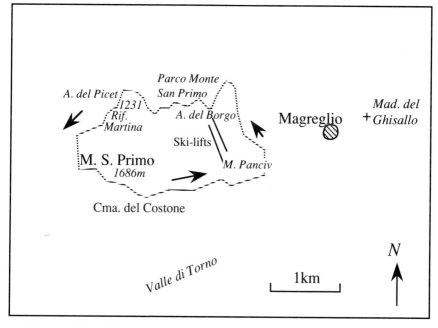

Parco Monte
San Primo

A. del Picet
1231
Rif.
Martina
A. del Borgo

Ski-lifts

Magreglio

Mad. del
+ Ghisallo

M. S. Primo
1686m

M. Panciv

Cma. del Costone

Valle di Torno

1km

N

d'Intelvi. The Rifugio is quite small - it has 18 beds - but the distinct advantage of a restaurant that is open from June until October.

Take the track behind the Rifugio that goes steeply up into woodland. Go through the woodland, beyond which open alp is reached and crossed to the top of Monte San Primo, the highest peak of the Triangola Lariano, as the area between the two arms of Lake Como is also sometimes called. From the peak the view extends to Switzerland's Monte Generoso, the Grigna, the Cornu di Canzo and the Apennines across the Lombardy Plain. Occasionally in Spring and Autumn, when the area is covered by the fog, Monte San Primo is covered with people taking photographs of the white cloud sea through which the taller peaks poke like islands. It is a magical sight.

On the summit there is a cross, the inscription on which translates as "Justice, Freedom, Peace, give your name to these". The radio mast is for the local Vigili del Fuoco, the forest fire wardens.

The return route from the summit depends upon the time you wish to spend on the walk. South from the top a route down the Vallone reaches the Val di Torno, locally famous for its spring flowers. But Val di Torno can be reached in much simpler fashion by taking the road from Sormano towards Nesso and parking near the bottom of the Monte Cippei ski lifts.

The better return is to go east along the summit ridge of Monte San Primo,

The Grigna and Resegone above a sea of clouds

passing Cima del Costone (1,616 metres - 5,300 feet) and then going down to the Bocchetta di Terre Biotte close to where the ski lifts have their top stations. From the Bocchetta take the track (signed for Route 39) which passes a prominent animal drinking *bolla* on its way to the top of Monte Ponciv (1,453 metres - 4,766 feet). Stay with the track as it turns north to reach Monte Forcella (1,329 metres - 4,359 feet). The way down from this last top is a blue run - at least it would be if you were on skis and there was enough snow on the hill - to the recently renewed Alpe del Brogo, a hostel now used by groups of schoolchildren who stay on "green" weeks to learn about the local environment and ecology or who come in winter to ski.

From Alpe del Brogo take the metalled road which leads back to the starting car park in about ten minutes.

Walk 19 Bellagio and Monte Nuvolone

Map No:	KOMPASS Carta Turistica (1:50,000) Sheet 91 (Lago di Como/Lago di Lugano)
Walking Time:	3 hours plus 2hrs .
Grade:	Easy
Highest Altitude:	Monte Nuvolone 1,094m (3,588 feet)
Lowest Altitude:	Guggiate 215m (705 feet)

Bellagio is the "Pearl of the Lake" a village thought by many to be not only the loveliest place on Lake Como, but also on any of the lakes. Indeed it has been suggested that Bellagio is the loveliest place in Italy, even in Europe. Given such hyperbole a visit is compulsory. You will not be disappointed. Whether the village is actually the loveliest of all is, of course, a matter of opinion. Of what there can be little doubt is that Bellagio is indeed a very pretty village, superbly set on one of the best parts of the lake. North of the village is Punta Spartivento, the point that splits the wind, not only an evocatively named spot, but one that offers an unrivalled view across the waters of Lake Como. Unrivalled by any other place at water level that is, for amongst other spots the high point of this walk offers a better view.

Bellagio's old port area, with its tight, narrow alleys and lakeside cafés is part of its attractiveness, but the village is famed as much for the ostentatious luxury of its villas. Villa Melzi d'Eryl is a masterpiece of Neo-Classical architecture and is set in fine, sculpted gardens. Villa Serbelloni is equally good.

The walk from Bellagio is excellent for its views, both of the village, the lake and the Val Perlo up which it climbs. The valley is of interest at the close-by level too, the flowers there drawing interested visitors each Spring.

The Walk

From Bellagio take the road for Como to reach Guggiate. From the little square close to S Andrea's church in that hamlet take the path marked as Route 2 which goes inland along the side of the Val Perlo. Cross the Perlo

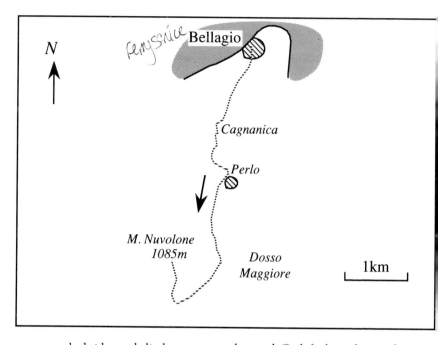

N

Bellagio
Cagnanica
Perlo
M. Nuvolone
1085m
Dosso
Maggiore
1km

stream by bridge and climb steps to reach a road. Go left along this to where it ends at a farm. There take a little track on the left to reach a pleasant terrace with trees. Pass Cagmamoca farm and go up between ivy-covered walls. Ignore the track to the right which goes to Vergonese, signed for Route 3, and continue towards the village of Perlo. The River Perlo is crossed by another bridge. It is a delightful stream at this point, the water flowing over glacial erratics, boulders brought to the site by glacial action during the last Ice Age. The village of Perlo is soon reached. It stands at 400 metres (1,312 feet), and is reached after about 30 minutes of walking.

From Perlo take the track signed for Route 4 going up steps to enter a fine chestnut wood. The Val Perlo becomes narrow now, the track winding as it gains height, and occasionally going up stepped sections. Relief comes at Begola where there are two old farms set on a level section of valley. There is also an old dovecote, now longer in use, but passed by our track as it approaches another deserted farm before climbing again to Brogno a village notable for the fine parkland around the Villa Mariani.

In Brogno ignore the track on the right that goes to Cascina Pelo, Route 5, and go down the road towards Bellagio to reach a mule track on the right. Take this, but leave it at the first bend on a path signed for Route 4 which goes along the valley side towards the farms of Seller (at 736 metres - 2,414 feet).

Near the farms the path reaches a forestry road which is followed over the river to a flat section of the valley where there is a fine, tiny chapel, the excellence of its position being augmented by the backdrop of Monte San Primo.

Ahead now is a slight rise: go over this and down to Rovenza (at 724 metres - 2,375 feet), a pleasant village with a fine fountain. Follow the village road for a short distance, branching off to the right on a track towards Taiana. Close to that village go right on a northward track that leads to a new building beyond which the path goes through a wood to reach a fine grassy plain at the end of which is Roccolo, a village offering a fine view over Lake Como, with Isola Comacina well defined, to the Val d'Intelvi. Monte Nuvolone, our next objective, is also well seen, a rounded, thickly vegetated mountain. Our route to it avoids the rocks on its eastern side.

Near a natural cave now transformed into chapel the path rises sharply between small outcrops. Beyond them leave the track for a path on the left that goes through woodland to reach the saddle between Monte Nuvolone's main summit, at 1,094 metres (3,588 feet), and a subsidiary summit at 1,058 metres (3,470 feet). Here there is an old hay barn. From the barn go right to reach the lower summit from where there is a superb view of Bellagio, Punta Spartivento and the lake. The climb to the highest point is barely worthwhile, thick vegetation largely obscuring the view, but the glacial erratics (massi erratici) littering the hillside do hold the interest as the walker plods the last few metres towards another tick in his "Munro-bagging" book of Italian peaks.

To return to Bellagio reverse the outward route, a journey which takes about two hours.

Walk 20 Valmadrera - Monte Rai - San Pietro al Monte - Civate

Map No:	KOMPASS Carta Turistica (1:50,000) Sheet 91 (Lago di Como/Lago di Lugano)
Walking Time:	4 hours
Grade:	Easy
Highest Altitude:	Monte Rai 1,259m (4,130 feet)
Lowest Altitude:	Valmadrera 234m (768 feet)

This walk is on a ridge south from the famous Corni di Canzo, the horns of Canzo that dominate the view across southern Lake Lecco. It follows easier ground than a climb on the ridge, however, passing through cultivated fields at first, then a woodland track, before breaking out on to open hillside. To descend a mule track is followed. The walk offers fine views, a close-up view of the area's interesting geology, and visits two fine, and historic, old churches.

The start is in Valmadrera an old silk milling village. The local area - and particularly Como, where the industry still thrives and silk ties and scarves are the stock tourist trade - was famous for its silk in Medieval times, and the Gavazzi mill buildings can still be seen, attached to Villa Gavazzi. The whole complex is an architectural delight, as well as being a site of historical interest, the mill chimney seemingly symmetrically set against the campanile beside the villa. Elsewhere in the village there is much of interest: S Antonio's church has twin bell towers, one dating from the late 16th century, the other a 90 metre (295 foot) campanile built early this century. Inside the church there are good paintings and sculptures. The church of S Rocco di Caserta also has fine frescoes, dating from the 16th century, while the church of S Martino is set on a hill up which leads a "Way of the Cross", the Way finishing at steps up to the church door.

The Walk

This walk is not precisely circular - unless you add on a mile or so of road

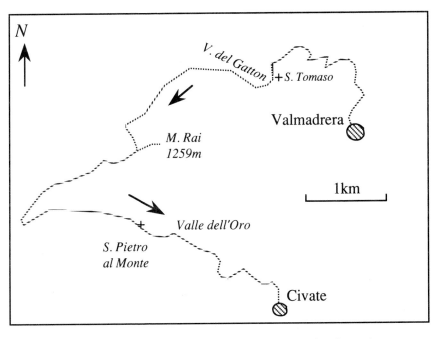

walking - but a bus runs from Civate, the end point, to Valmadrera, the start. It is usually best to take the bus first. Then all you have to do is walk...

From Valmadrera, follow signs to the hamlet of Belvedere, named for its excellent view, a little to the north. From there take the road which is closed to the traffic, towards the little chapel titled VARS. Now follow the yellow, red and white waymarks (indicating Route 3 of the local Alpine Association who we have to thank for waymarking the route throughout) that goes to the left through fields to the abandoned hamlet of Mondonico. Continue along the signed route, crossing the Val Gatton and its stream, to San Tomaso, a hamlet set among old chestnut trees.

From San Tomaso the waymarkers remain, but the route changes to No. 1, taking you into the wooded Val Molinata whose stream is somewhat exaggeratedly called Inferno. The route contours around the valley at first, but soon climbs up its left side - ie. the stream is on your left hand - changing from a track to a path. Look out for a prominent spring, the Acqua del Tufo, which you will find soon after the Val Molinata has swung left to reveal Monte Prasanto at its head. There is a short climb after the spring, at the end of which the path swings through a semi-circle to cross the by now tiny stream. Continue up the right side of the valley, ie. with the stream on your right side.

After the wood ends the path goes up steep pasture (alp) to reach the Bochetta di San Mizo where you will find a crucifix. The literal translation of bocchetta is mouthpiece, as on an instrument, but it is frequently used for small caves and hollows. From the cross the top of Monte Rai is obvious and straightforwardly reached. From the top the view is magnificent, though inevitably dominated by the Corni di Canzo to the north, and the lakes of Lecco and Annone. Below, to the south, is the Valle dell'Oro (the Valley of Gold) down which our return route will go, and the final village of Civate. The area close to the top of the peak is a favourite haunt of amateur geologists because of its particular form of dolomitic rock - Monte Prasanto is even more interesting in this respect - and of plant lovers, the dolomitic rock giving the area a virtually unique flora.

To descend, return to the Bocchetta di San Mizo, and take the path going west (left) - Route No. 10 - to reach the transmission aerial of SIP, the Italian telephone company. From there the path descends easily to the Rifugio Marize Consiglieri, a mountain hut of SEC, a walker's club of Ciavate. The hut is also occasionally known as Culmen, a name which can occasionally be found on signs, but this correctly refers to this part of the slopes of Monte Cornizzolo, the peak we have reached by traversing from Monte Rai across the head of the Valle dell'Oro. You will rapidly notice that the hut can also be reached by road - from Eupilio, a small village complex on the northern shore of Lake Pusiano. If you are faced with walkers recently emerged from cars, exude an air of quiet, superior satisfaction. The view from the southern flank of Monte Cornizzolo is almost as good as that from Monte Rai, with the Lombardy Plain laid out beyond the small lakes of the Erba valley.

From the rifugio take the track - still Route No. 10 - going down the Valle dell'Oro, south-east from Cornizzolo. The route, at first, is through pasture with some low shrubs, but after the delightfully named Fountain Alp it becomes wooded again. This is superb walking country, and in no time, it seems, you reach the ancient basilica of San Pietro al Monte and the oratory of S Benedetto.

The complex was built in the 8th century by the Lombard King Desidero as a thanksgiving to God for the survival of his son after a hunting accident. The King endowed the buildings as a Benedictine monastery, though it is many years since there were monks here.

S Pietro's is invariably open in Summer, but at other times it is wise to call for the key at the caretaker's house in Civate - ask at the church or at the Tourist Office in Lecco for details. The basilica was rebuilt in the 11th century when the twin apses were created. The entrance door is reached up an ancient stone stairway. The basilica has two apses, a very rare painted and

San Pietro al Monte

stuccoed crypt, dating from the 11th century, the art work portraying Christ's Death, Resurrection and Return, and beautiful frescoes. The Oratory of S Benedetto holds an equally rare work of art, a painted altar from the 12th century.

From the basilica and oratory take the steep track under the old monastic arch to reach an old paved mule track, which takes you along the Golden Valley's river to Cascina Oro and on to Pozzo. Bear left there on to a lane that leads down to Civate. In the village be sure to visit the church of S Calcero, a fine frescoed church which was once a place of pilgrimage. Several - now empty - silver and marble boxes that anciently contained saintly relics can still be seen, as can the most important relic, some chain and keys once owned by St Peter, formerly held at the basilica of S Pietro, but now kept in a Gothic shrine here at S Calcero.

From Civate those who have left their cars in Valmadrera will catch the bus back to that village.

Walk 21   Resegone di Lecco

Map No:	KOMPASS Carta Turistica (1:50,000) Sheet 105 (Lecco - Valle Brembana)
Walking Time:	5 hours, but a shorter variation (3 hours) possible
Grade:	Medium
Highest Altitude:	Rifugio Azzoni 1,860m (6,101 feet)
Lowest Altitude	Funivia Lower Station 602m (1,975 feet), but the Top Station 1,300m (4,264 feet) is the shorter walk is followed.

Lecco, at the southern end of the eastern arm of Lake Como, is a large, modern town, second only to Como itself, but still has an old-fishing-port quarter and surroundings of such scenic splendour that its modernity is easily forgiven. Of its particular attractions special note should be made of the Visconti Bridge - the most southern of the two, ie. the furthest from Lake Como - that has been renovated to look much as it did when Azzone Visconti had it built over the Adda in 1336. Originally it had drawbridge sections on both ends, but, with modern traffic, it was not thought reasonable to restore these!

Within the town there are statues of Garibaldi who liberated the area, and of Lecco's most famous son, Alessandro Manzoni, a writer whose book, *il Promesso Spossi*, translated as "The Betrothed" and dealing with the Spanish occupation of Lecco in the 17th century, was described by Sir Walter Scott as the best book ever written. The villa known as "Il Caleotto", in which Manzoni spent much of his early life, as well as parts of his later life, is now a shrine to the writer. Known now as Villa Manzoni, it is in Via Amendola, which can be reached by continuing in a straight line after crossing the Visconti Bridge into Lecco.

As an interesting addition to Lecco's pride in Manzoni, each year in late May or early June the Pedalata Manzoniana is held, a 30 kilometre (19 mile) cycle ride that visits all the places mentioned in "The Betrothed" as having been visited by main characters, Renzo and Lucia.

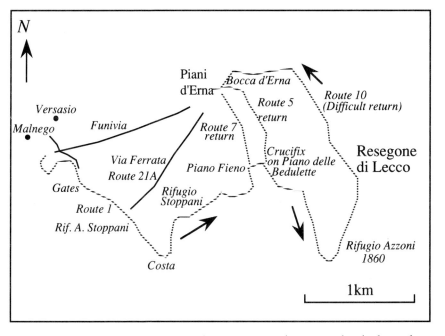

The Resegone, or Monte Serrada to give it its alternative, but little used name, is mentioned in Manzoni's book. Our walk climbs to its highest point along a straightforward path that needs care after heavy rain. If you are visiting on a good weekend day in summer, be prepared for company, the Resegone is popular with climbers from Lecco and Bergamo. Lecco, in particular, is proud of its reputation as a training ground for famous Italian alpinists - the *Lecco Ragni*, spiders - and many aspirant Bonattis can be found along the way.

The Walk

Park at the bottom station of the funivia that rises to Piani d'Erna below the rock faces of the Resegone. Go right of the station, dropping down through trees to a path. Go left along this to a road, and right along the road to gates at its end. To the left here is a mule track: take this (Route 1, red and white splashes). To the left after about 800 metres the path (Route 22) to the base of the Pizzo d'Erna and the Via Ferrata followed by Walk 21A is reached. For the purposes of this walk we ignore that turning, continuing to a large albergo (inn/hotel), near where Route 4 joins from the right, and the alpine hut complex of Costa.

Here, leave the mule track and go up steps, on the left between the huts, to reach a steep track that leads to the Rifugio Stoppani. The walk continues by going up the track behind the Rifugio, a track that goes past a spring (Acqua del Cop) and crosses a small stream. Ignore Route 5 that leaves for Passo del Fo on the right and bear to reach Piano Fieno. Go up into woodland from this small piece of flat land, ignoring tracks on the left and right - most prominently Route 5 coming in from the left, from Bocca d'Erna - to reach the Crucifix on Piano delle Bedulette.

From the cross Route 1 goes south-east into the mountain gully of Val Comera climbing up to the convenient resting point at the Baite di Serrada. Bear right here over the Piano Serrada, beyond which the path rises again to reach Passo delle Sibretta on the Resegone ridge. Ahead now Route 11 comes in from the right just before the path reaches Rifugio Azzoni, set just a few metres down from the huge cross on to top of Punta Cermenati, at 1,875 metres (6,150 feet) the highest of the Resegone towers. The Rifugio - or the summit for that matter, the summit being easily reached unless you are early or late in the season and the snow is still lying on the last climb - offers a superb panorama, both beautiful and interesting, with the little lakes of Brianza, the Grigna, the mountains of the northern Bergamo valleys and the Apennines all being visible. The Rifugio has 18 beds and is open daily in August, at week-ends in the other months from May to October and occasionally, depending on the weather, in the remaining months. Plan your trip wisely, therefore, and the asymmetrically roofed hut offer will offer refreshment and a good place to contemplate the downward route.

The easiest route, in the sense of distance and height loss, is Route 10, which goes to the north-east of the Resegone towers directly to Piani d'Erna and the funivia top station. However, this route is impegnativi (literally, demanding) and should not be taken lightly. Far easier is to reverse the outward walk to the crucifix at Piano delle Bedulette and to follow Route 5 from there, or to continue to Piano Fieno and from there follow Route 7. Either of these routes is straightforward and reaches the wide Bocca d'Erna below the funivia top station.

To shorten the walk considerably - and to remove the first 700 metres (2,296 feet) or so of ascent - take the funivia to the top station and follow Route 7 to Piano Fieno, continuing as above to Rifugio Azzoni, taking Route 5 from Piano delle Bedulette on the return leg.

Walk 21A   Ferrata Pizzo d'Erna

Map No:	KOMPASS Carta Turistica (1:50,000) Sheet 105 (Lecco/Valle Brembana)
Walking Time:	2 hours, but variable
Grade:	Via Ferrata (see Notes below)
Highest Altitude:	Pizzo d'Erna 1,362m (4,467 feet)
Lowest Altitude:	Funivia Lower Station 602m (1,975 feet)

All over the Dolomites the Italians have fixed some of the steeper faces with wire "handrail" ropes, chains, ladders, pegs and rungs in order to allow mountain walkers with a head for heights to reach tops - and to scale faces - that were previously the preserve of the pure rock climbers. These routes are known as Vie Ferrata - Iron Roads, an appropriate name. Many will decry the ironmongery and the desecration that it brings, but in truth there is an awful lot of rock in northern Italy and not that many Vie Ferrata (by comparison). In addition the routes invariably start from high on the hill, so that they are rarely overlooked: from a mile or two away, or a thousand or so feet below the ladders are barely visible - difficult to pick out rather than difficult to ignore.

This book is about walking, and in the main covers country where the walker is king. But to the east of Lake Como's eastern arm (Lake Lecco) the rock towers of the Grigna and the Resegone are ideal for the iron routes. BEFORE EMBARKING ON THIS ROUTE PLEASE READ THE NOTES BELOW.

Vie Ferrata (in Italian vie is the plural of via) are dangerous if not approached correctly. Some sections go up vertical, or even overhanging rock, so that if your safety precautions fail and you slip, you will die.

To embark on a Via Ferrata you must be sure of your ability to come to terms with exposure of the route: some of the climbs are many hundreds (even thousands) of feet long and can have long sections of extreme exposure. Retreat is feasible, but may be complicated - not least if there are people coming up the route behind you!

The climber must be well equipped. Sections of the route will be on rock, so boots with a reasonable sole are necessary. But the boots should not be too

Via Ferrata Pizzo D'Erna

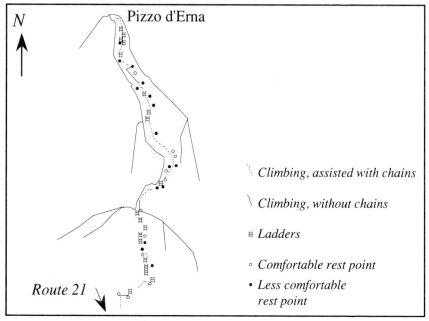

N

Pizzo d'Erna

Route 21

⟍ *Climbing, assisted with chains*

⟍ *Climbing, without chains*

Ħ *Ladders*

∘ *Comfortable rest point*

• *Less comfortable rest point*

big: a big mountain boot (such as a plastic outer boot) will give you grief on the ladder pitches. The climber should wear a climbing harness. Indeed, if a Vie Ferrata kit is not used a climbing harness is virtually essential. To the harness you should fix one length of rope so that there are two equal lengths, about one metre long hanging from it. To the end of each length a karabiner is attached. There must be two karabiners. The ladders and ropes are attached to the rock by pitons or spikes at regular intervals: when the climber starts up the route he attaches both karabiners to the wire - if there is a section of chain to pull on, or if there is a ladder, there will be a wire rope running up the side of it for the karabiners. Then, at each fixing point of ladder or chain, the climber transfers one karabiner above the spike, following this by transferring the other. At no time therefore is the climber un-belayed. This procedure should be carried out at all times. If a climber does slip he will fall back to the last spike, then a metre or so past it, then stop very quickly. The high fall factor of such a descent means potential injury. It is important therefore that the climber wears a harness to distribute the load, or (preferably, and) a widget developed by continental Vie Ferrata climbers. This is a "knuckleduster" of metal through the holes of which the rope going off to the karabiners passes, the twists and turns helping to absorb the fall energy.

I have observed solo climbers on Vie Ferrata on several occasions. As with

108

A ladder pitch on the Via Ferrata

all forms of climbing the greater the commitment the greater the buzz, but for safety's sake it is best to go in pairs. A rucsac will be needed to carry life's necessities - there being few cafés on the vertical sections! - and these should include a section of climbing rope. A full 45 or 50 metre rope is not needed, but a 25 metre length, together with some belay slings will be handy. Some of the route have vertical sections where the karabiner transfer system is difficult or impossible. These sections should be climbed using the rock climbing technique of leader and second-man with the normal belaying.

Finally, many climbers on the routes do not wear helmets. There is no proscriptive advice here, but do remember that most of these routes are on limestone which is notoriously loose. And absolutely finally, remember that in the northern Italian hills, where cold air and warm air are often meeting across a high mountain ridge, thunderstorms are relatively common and can arrive quickly. If one approaches, your Iron Road will become a lightning conductor. Move away from it as fast and as far as possible.

If all the above makes Vie Ferrata sound like the abode of supermen, please think again. They offer superb ways into wonderful country and are within range of any reasonable fit, sensible walker with a guaranteed head for heights. The route offered here is a straightforward one which, though it has several vertical ladder pitches, some of which are long, has limited technical requirements and will be within the scope of anyone with some climbing experience and ability. To have a look at it before trying it out, take the funivia to the Piani d'Erna, the top ladder pitches being visible from the cable car as it nears the top station. That is another reason for trying this route first - it finishes at the Piani, allowing a quick walk to the café and a ride down in the cable car.

The Via Ferrata

Follow Walk 21 from the lower funivia station to the turn off for Route 22 mentioned in the description of that route. Follow Route 22 as it goes up through woodland to reach a steep and miserable scree slope. At the top of this is the Via Ferrata. The route is shown in the accompanying topo guide, on which all the rest points and their reasonableness are given. The walk-in starts at 602 metres (1,975 feet), but the Via Ferrata starts at about 750 metres, so that the change in altitude on it is about 600 metres (about 2,000 feet).

From the top take the tourist-worn path to the café and funivia top station.

Walk 22   The Grignone from Esino Lario

Map No:	KOMPASS Carta Turistica (1:50,000) Sheet 91 (Lago di Como/Lago di Lugano)
Walking Time:	6 hours
Grade:	Difficult
Highest Altitude:	Grigna Settentrionale (Grignone) 2,409m (7,902 feet)
Lowest Altitude:	Vo di Moncodeno 1,460m (4,789 feet)

On the eastern shore of Lake Lecco is the Grigna, a limestone range stretching from just north of Lecco to the Valsassina, a wide valley going inland from Bellano, a lake-shore town famous for its Orrido, a deep-cut gorge reached by rope bridges and walkways.

Though the Grigna is the western end of the Orobie Alps it is a displaced part of the Dolomites, a mass of rock with towers and sweeping arêtes that would not look at all out of place near Cortina or Belluno. The routes on the range are also similar: uncompromising routes with exposure and wire ropes, bare rock and large changes of altitude. The range is traversed by the Alta Via delle Grigne a "high road" that is waymarked throughout and offers what is without doubt the best four day outing in the Lakes area. For those with less time there are caves to explore in the lower reaches of the limestone and acres of alpine flowers. The Grigna has two chief peaks: to the north is Grigna Settentrionale, the highest peak at 2,409 metres (7,902 feet), a peak known more usually as Grignone, the big Grigna. To the south is Grigna Meridionale, 2,184 metres (7,164 feet) known, no surprise this, as Grignetta, the little Grigna.

Our route climbs the highest peak, but uses a high car park to reduce the amount of climbing required. The start point is reached from Esino Lario, a tourist resort in both summer and winter, and called - chiefly by the local tourist office - the "village of the sun". Take the road to Cainallo, and continue to Vo di Moncodeno where parking is easy. The route is waymarked throughout with splashes of red and yellow paint, the route numbers being given at each fork in the path. As noted in the text, however, the waymarking

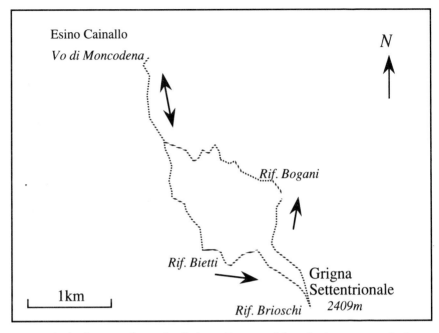

Esino Cainallo
Vo di Moncodena

Rif. Bogani

Rif. Bietti

Grigna
Settentrionale
2409m

Rif. Brioschi

N

1km

is a little devious above the Rifugio Bogani, although there is very little danger of becoming lost.

The Walk

Take the track at the back of the parking area - Route No. 25 - a wide track with an expanding view of the Grigna. After about 30 minutes of walking you will reach a fork. Follow Route No. 25, an undulating track that leads to another fork. Go right on Route No. 24 through woodland and the Bocchetta di Prada to reach a path that hugs the steep, rocky face, to the left, that falls from the Grigna ridge. Follow the path to a curious natural feature, a rock arch - the Porta Prada - within which a crucifix has been set up. It is typically Italian that there should be such a cross, the significance of which is usually limited to a need to "humanise" the feature.

Beyond the arch the path is obvious but occasionally devious as it crosses steep ground. Relief comes with the sighting of Rifugio Bietti, where on my visit the guardian found it is hard to believe that the Englishman wanted water or something else soft rather than a glass of wine, despite the temperature being at the dripping sweat level.

Even on the hottest day there will be respite on the next walk section. Go

The rock arch

behind the hut and attack the ridge by way of the zig-zag path up to the Grigna ridge. The temperature drops with each metre climbed, and when the ridge is reached there is invariably a cooling breeze. Go right and up the ridge path towards the now visible summit.

Close to the top the path goes across the rocky face of the high peak to reach a shallow scrape up which a chain is followed or climbed up the final few metres. Go left to reach a chapel set astride the ridge, a glass structure that concentrates the view. Beyond is the summit hut, Rifugio Brioschi, open all year and with 32 beds, food, drink (and even a telephone) and the summit itself, complete with another cross. From the top there is a beautiful panorama from the Bernina Alps to Monte Rosa, and including the Matterhorn. To the south is the Lombardy Plain, with Milan beneath its foggy shroud. On very clear days - so I am told - Florence is visible.

Return along the ridge to the chains and descend. At the end do not reverse the outward route to the ridge, but continue down a path that is obvious at first - where else is there to go? - but becomes more difficult to follow once more level ground is reached. Do not despair, the way is always down and all routes are funnelled towards the Rifugio Bogani (once the Rifugio Monza). The reason for the funnelling is, of course, geographical, a single route - Route No. 25 - traversing the impressive face that falls away

The summit cross

from the final section of the Grignone's ridge. This track reaches the fork where we branched right on the outward journey. From there, reverse the outward journey back to Vo di Moncodeno.

From Como to Garda

Between Lake Como and Lake Garda, the most easterly of the big lakes, is a land of real mountains split by deep valleys. Strictly this is not our area, as it is a little removed from the lake areas, but few walkers visiting the lakes will ignore all that wilderness.

The most well-known of the valleys in the area is the Valtellina. The Valtellina has always been important in Italian history, for while most of the alpine valleys, and all of the passes, run north-south the Valtellina - the valley of the river Adda - lies predominantly east-west. As a consequence many of the alpine passes end in the Valtellina, so that control of the valley gave control of many passes. In addition the Adda flows into Lake Como which gave the defenders of the valley quick access to the Lombardy plain. The valley is famous for its wines - Grumello and Sassella to name just two - the vineyards for which are frame grown and are to be seen everywhere. It also has great scenic beauty, the lower alpine slopes bearing woods of oak and chestnut, while higher there are rhododendron, firs and larch, and everywhere the usual rich and diverse alpine flora. It is also an area rich in minerals and has attracted crystal hunters for many years.

At the centre of the valley is Sondrio, a fine city, though the most famous towns are the winter sport resorts of Aprica and - up a side valley - Bormio and Livigno. On the northern side of the valley near its eastern end is the Stelvio National Park, one of the best in Italy.

South of the Valtellina are the high Orobie Alps, from which valleys drain southward towards the Lombardy Plain. On the Plain is Bergamo, one of the finest Renaissance cities in Italy, a city that should be on the itinerary of every visitor to the area. Bergamo is actually two cities, the lower one being a modern town, the upper one being the one that should be visited.

The upper city is fully walled, the walls having been completed by the Venetians in the late 16th century, when the city was the Venetian Republic's western bastion and so entry to it can only be made through the ancient gates and cars are, to all intents and purposes, excluded. Four gates exist, and, in addition a funivia runs up from the lower city. This is an excellent way to approach the upper city. You climb on board the rack railway and when you get out you are several metres higher, and 400 years further back in time.

Two valleys end at Bergamo. Val Seriana's lower section is wide bottomed, with gently sloping sides that allow easy farming on fertile soil. Higher up, the valley is beautifully unspoilt, its alpine pastures offering excellent walking in cool surroundings and with wonderful views.

Val Brembana has a curious geography that before the advent of modern road engineering meant that it was virtually cut off from the outside world. To the north, that is at its head, there are high peaks without passes, and ridges of these peaks run not only down the east and west sides of the valley, but weave east and west at the southern end to produce a difficult exit for the river, through the "straits" as they are called. As a consequence, until about 1600 there were only two passes into the valley, and neither of them was particularly easy. Not surprisingly the valley folk evolved a rich mixture of dialect, culture and architecture which, while it has not survived intact into the modern era, does at least colour

Further east is Val Camonica in which lies Lake Iseo, the fifth biggest of the lakes. The high ground above the lake is of limited value to the walker, though any visitor to the area will want to see the erosion pyramids near Zone, a village above the eastern shore. Uneven glacial erosion, caused by the layering of the strata, has created eerie pillars of earthy conglomerate, some tens of metres high. They look, at first glance like termite nests, but invariably they are topped by a granite boulder, precariously balanced. Though not unique in Alpine Europe this collection of pyramids is reckoned to be the finest and offer one of the most unusual views in the lakes' area. Equally entertaining are the *bögns* of Castro and Zorzino at the north-western end of the lake. The *bögns* are huge sheets of limestone plunging vertically from the slopes of Monte Clemo into the lake.

For many, however, Val Camonica is visited in order to view the rock carvings. The valley became famous when the first of the carvings - engraved into the relatively soft Permian sandstone - was discovered, a fame that grew rapidly to international status when the extent and age of the works was realised. Today almost 200,000 individual works have been catalogued, the engravings showing a range of subjects, but chiefly hunting scenes, scenes from ordinary life and religious themes. One individual rock, the Naquane Rock, in the Parco della Incisioni Rupestiri - the National Rock Engravings Park - has 900 figures carved on it. In age, the carvings cover some 8,000 years from the Neolithic era through to Roman times, a truly amazing depiction of life as civilisation dawned. In 1979 UNESCO gave the site international protection as being of world importance. The National Park is centred on Capo di Ponte, where the study centre for the carvings was set up in the sixties.

In this section of the book there are three walks which explore the high ground of this inter-lake area. None of the walks visits Val Camonica. In that valley it is better that the walker visits the National Park and explores the area at his own speed.

Walk 23   Angeloga Lake and Pass in Valchiavenna

Map No:	KOMPASS Carta Turistica (1:50,000) Sheet 92 (Chiavenna/Val Bregaglia)
Walking Time:	3 hours to Rifugio Chiavenna 5 hours to Passo di Angeloga
Grade:	Medium to the Rifugio Difficult to the Pass
Highest Altitude:	Rifugio Chiavenna 2,044m (6,704 feet) Passo di Angeloga 2,391m (7,842 feet)
Lowest Altitude:	Soste 1,442m (4,730 feet)

The S Giacomo Valley, that runs from Chiavenna to Passo dello Spluga, the Spluga Pass, through the famous tourist resorts of Madesimo and Campodolcino, is normally called Valchiavenna.

Within the valley the walk to Lake Angeloga and the Rifugio Chiavenna and on to the Angeloga Pass to see the Val di Lei is one of the most famous and also one of the most beautiful. It is an alpine route, the whole of the outward walk having views with a backdrop of the peaks on the Italian-Swiss border. The route starts high and goes higher: it is a mountainous route, so take appropriate precautions and be sure to carry the correct equipment.

From Campodolcino take the road to Fraciscio and drive through the village. At the final fork go right for the hamlet of Soste. Park just beyond the bar, where the road becomes a wide mule track.

The Walk

Take the mule track, signed for both the Rifugio Chiavenna and the Passo di Angeloga, a track that becomes more difficult in the Val Rabbiosa. Soon the track reaches, and follows, the Rabbiosa river which adds to the scenic magnificence of the route. Follow the track as it winds uphill between rocks and bushes, avoiding the rocky wall that supports the Angeloga lake. After some consistent climbing, altitude and effort requiring stops that at least have the virtue of allowing the scenery to be admired at length, the ground

117

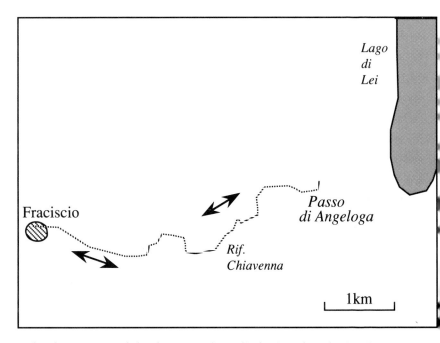

Lago di Lei

Fraciscio

Passo di Angeloga

Rif. Chiavenna

1km

levels out to reveal the shining surface of Lake Angeloga (at 2,039 metres - 6,688 feet). It is not too far now to the mountain hut of Angeloga and Rifugio Chiavenna (at 2,044 metres - 6,704 feet). The Rifugio can sleep 78 people and is open at weekends from June to October, and every day in August. It is run by the Chiavenna group of the CAI (Italian Alpine Club).

This really is the most beautiful place, with the clear water of the lake, the green of the flat land beside it, the whole looked over by the big peaks of Pizzo Stella and Pizzo Peloso with the Ponciagna Glacier running down their eastern side. From the Rifugio a splendid, and very easy track goes to Motte, reaching it in about two hours, from where are the ski lifts to Madesimo, which is connected by bus to Campodolcino.

Our walk continues to the Passo di Angeloga, going north on a winding track behind the Rifugio. The way is up a gully cut by the outfall stream of Lago Nero - the black lake - and passage is occasionally assisted by wire ropes, though these are never too difficult. The Lake Nero dam is reached: follow the path along the lake edge, under the imposing wall of Pizzo Groppera. Ahead now the path passes several smaller lakes before Passo di Angeloga (at 2,391 metres - 7,842 feet) is reached, its top marked by a wooden cross. From the Pass the view along the Val di Lei is magnificent. The lake of the valley is a strange, narrow strip of water which lies wholly within Italy even though

The lake and Rifugio Chiavenna

the dam at its far end lies within Switzerland. This is a curious quirk of political geography, as the border between the countries lies on the top of the eastern edge of the valley, coming down into the valley only to run along the two sides of the dam before going east back on to the ridge. This means that not only the lake, but the outfall river on the northern side of the dam lie in Italy. Very strange.

To return to the Rifugio Chiavenna you can reverse the outward route, or take a poorly signed path going left after the first lake passed (on the return from the Pass that is). This path stays above Lake Caldera before going directly down towards Lake Angeloga and the Rifugio. This route is called the Cow Path because it was anciently used by cow-herders taking their animals over the Pass to the lowland pastures of the Val di Lei.

From Rifugio Chiavenna it is possible to climb Pizzo Stella (3,163 metres - 10,375 feet) in about 3 hours. It has the lure of being a 10,000 foot peak, and of offering stupendous views. But it is a long, hard climb - perhaps another day....

To return to Soste from the Rifugio reverse the outward route.

Walk 24   The Twin Lakes, Val Brembana

Map No:	KOMPASS Carta Turistica (1:50,000) Sheet 104 (Foppolo/Valle Seriana)
Walking Time:	7 hours (but spread over two days if required)
Grade:	Difficult (but medium if completed in two days)
Highest Altitude:	Rifugio Laghi Gemelli 1,968m (6,455 feet)
Lowest Altitude:	Roncobello 1,007m (3,303 feet)

This walk, which starts from Carona, is the classic walk of the upper reaches of the Val Brembana, a walk through a country of woods, alpine lakes and rare beauty. It can be completed in one long day, but to savour its delights it is better to complete it in two, spending a night in the Rifugio Laghi Gemelli, the hut of the twin lakes, before continuing to Roncobello which is connected by bus to Carona by way of Piazza Brembana, the most important village in the Brembana valley.

The Rifugio Laghi Gemelli - owned by the Bergamo branch of the CAI (Italian Alpine Club) - has 70 beds and in summer operates more as a small hotel than a mountain hut, so accommodation should not be a problem. To be on the safe side ring first, on 0345/71212

If the walk is completed in two days the requirements of each are:-
Day 1: a distance of 7 kms (4 miles) and a climb of 870m (2,854 feet).
Day 2: a distance of 13 kms (8 miles), a climb of 174m (571 feet) and a descent of 1,135m (3,723 feet).

It is possible that strong walkers making an early start will complete the walk. However, when it is borne in mind that this is high country, where the carrying of reserve equipment, wet weather gear etc. is compulsory rather than advisable, and a return journey from Roncobello to Carona is necessary, then the possibility of a completing the walk over two days must be strongly considered

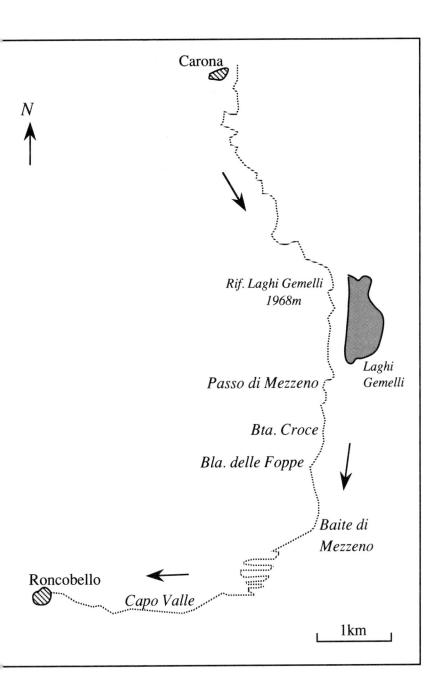

Carona

N

*Rif. Laghi Gemelli
1968m*

*Laghi
Gemelli*

Passo di Mezzeno

Bta. Croce

Bla. delle Foppe

*Baite di
Mezzeno*

Roncobello

Capo Valle

1km

The Walk

Day 1: The walk starts from the southern shore of Lake Carona, beside the bar where the coffee will taste better for being the last cup before several hours of good, but coffee-free, walking. The walk follows Route 211, a well-signed path that is easy to follow, but occasionally steep as it rises through woodland towards the high slopes. After a level section of the walk, where the path goes under the ENEL (Italian Electricity) power lines there is a particularly steep section to reach a junction of paths. Here the Sentiero delle Orobie goes off to the left - towards the Rifugio Calvi - while we continue up the valley to reach the bottom of the Lake Marcio dam. The path winds up the right side of this to reach the west side of the lake, at 1,841 metres (6,038 feet). Pause here to contemplate the view back along the route, framed by the peaks close to Foppolo, and of nearby Pizzo dell'Orto and Monte del Tonale.

On the far side of the lake, where the ENEL cableway has its top station - the cableway is not open to the public - descend a little to reach the track that follows the northern shore of Lake Casere. The stream flowing down Val di Gorno - the combined outfall streams of Lake Colombo, above and to the east, and the Gemelli lakes, above and north, and our next destination - is crossed by bridge, beyond which the track continues south-east, passing close to a large building set in fine, wide pasture. From here it is only a short way to the Rifugio Laghi Gemelli, the hut standing close to the dam built prior to the 1939-45 War. Close to the Rifugio there is a tiny chapel, a gentle touch.

The Rifugio - set high, in wild country softened by pine trees - is an excellent starting point for walks, so if you are staying the night consider the walk to Lake Colombo, a round trip of about an hour and an ideal way to round off the day.

Day 2: Go south from the Rifugio, taking Route 225 along the western shore of what is now, after damming, not two but one lake. This shoreline walk is one of the highlights of the trip, the view across the lake and towards Monte Spondone to the right (west) being magnificent. About two-thirds of the way along the lake you will reach a fork. The path to the left goes over Passo dei Laghi Gemelli (the Pass of the Twin Lakes) to Rifugio Alpe Orte in Val Canole, but our way is to the right.

The path goes gently up to reach Passo di Mezzeno (at 2,142 metres - 7,026 feet) from where the spectacular, high peak of Pizzo Arera can be seen to the south. Beyond the pass a good track goes down to the Baite Croce, set where the ground levels off. Follow the path through fine flower-decked alpine meadow to reach another mountain hut, the Baite delle Foppe. From

Rifugio Laghi Gemelli

here the track zig-zags down and east, reaching a small aqueduct taking water down into the valley. Follow the aqueduct for a while to reach the Baite di Mezzeno (at 1,591 metres - 5,218 feet) where a road down into the valley starts. Take this, passing through a beautiful pine forest, as the road loses height by winding down the hillside in approved alpine fashion. Soon the village of Capo Valle is reached from where 15 minutes of walking brings you to Roncobello and the end of a glorious two days.

Walk 25   The Three Valleys' Track

Map No:	KOMPASS Carta Turistica (1:50,000) Sheet 71 (Adamello/La Presanella)
Walking Time:	Total time: 12 hours a) from Vezza d'Oglio to Rifugio alla Cascata: 1 hour b) from Rifugio alla Cascata to Rifugio Orizio: 4 hours c) from Rifugio Orizio to Ponte di Legno: 5 hours d) from Ponte di Legno to Vezza d'Oglio: 2 hours
Grade:	Medium
Highest Altitude:	Rifugio Orizio 2,100m (6,888 feet)
Lowest Altitude	Vezza d'Oglio 1,080m (3,542 feet)

Between Lakes Como and Garda there is mountainous country split by long valleys only one of which holds a large lake, the Val d'Oglio holding Lake Iseo. The valleys run north-south and two, Val Seriana and Val Brembana, are excellent, and should be explored. To the north the Valtellina runs east-west, and is dotted with resorts now becoming better known to the winter sport enthusiast, Aprica, Teglio and, in a side valley, Tonale and Bormio. The Valtellina forms the southern boundary of the Stelvio National Park, one of the small number of Italian National Parks set up to preserve scenic magnificence and a fine range of animals, birds and plants. The Stelvio is famous for its chamois and ibex, and for its golden eagles. South of the Park, and the Valtellina, is the Adamello, a huge mountain area that is most distinctly non-Dolomite despite its closeness to the Brenta. Adamello itself is 3,554 metres (11,657 feet) high and is definitely not the place for the average walker. North of the highest ground valleys drain the permanent snows into the Valtellina. Three of those valleys lie within the Adamello Natural Park, almost an extension of the Stelvio and sharing much of its wildlife, if not its status. This walk crosses three of those valleys, linking Vezza

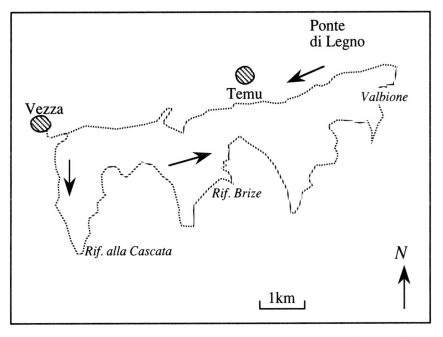

d'Oglio, set where the Oglio valley meets the Valtellina, with Ponte di Legno. It is a long walk, the right length for a weekend, though the component parts can be walked as sections, and the overall time can be reduced by travelling back from Ponte to Vezza by bus.

The Walk

The walk has been waymarked, and is maintained, along the whole of its length by the CAI (the Italian Alpine Club). From Vezza to Valbione, very much the largest part of the walk, the track is numbered 72. From Valbione to Ponte follow Route 10, and if you are completing the return by foot follow Route 41.

Though it visits high places and is, in parts, rugged the track is straightforward and offers wonderful views. Because of the height mountain equipment is necessary. However, escape from the route is also straightforward, there being many possibilities for to reach the main valley from the side valleys that are crossed.

Leave Vezza d'Oglio on the road to the Val Paghera along which the scenery soon takes on what will become a familiar appearance, with large woods of red firs and larches. When you get to the Ponte Scalvino, the bridge over the Val Paghera's outflow stream, you will see your first CAI sign for Route 72. Here too there is car parking for those not wishing to spend two days on the route, but anxious to sample the delights of the first day, and a fine picnic site. Follow Route 72 to the refuge/hotel of Rifugio alla Cascata.

Those wishing to limit their walking should follow Route 21 from the Rifugio which, in about an hour, leads to the Piano d'Aviolo where is another Rifugio (Rifugio Aviolo) and the beautiful alpine lake, Lago d'Aviolo, that gives the hut its name.

Back on the main track, follow the signs for Route 72 from Rifugio alla Cascata to Baite di Pornina - a baite is a small mountain hut. The terrace of Pornina offers a beautiful panoramic view over valleys and mountains. It is the last expansive view for a while as the track now descends through dark woods towards the Vallaro valley (Val di Vallaro), a pleasant valley littered with farms and rifugios. Escape from Val di Vallaro is by way of a variant to Route 72 which heads north to Stadolina, just a mile or two from Vezza d'Oglio.

The track continues up-valley on Route 72 before going east around a rocky arm of the Adamello (Monte Calvo) to reach Rifugio Orizio. This Rifugio is private, so if you wish to use it you will need to arrange things beforehand. Telephone 0364-94196 to do so.

The escape route from the Rifugio is straightforward: head north for Temu which is reached in about 1 hour.

From Rifugio Orizio the track goes down into Valle dell'Avio, the Avio Valley one of the earliest in Italy to have been dammed for hydro-electric purposes. Those with more time, or those using the track for a day trip, can go up the valley to see the three artificial lakes created by the hydro-electric scheme.

Cross the Avio's stream by way of the delightful wooden bridge close to the cable car bottom station - the top station is beside the smaller of the three lakes - and follow the signs for the Baite di Mezzullo. The track is fairly level here, and offers wide panoramas to the north as it contours around this final arm of the Adamello. From the baite continue to Valbione. In winter there is an operating chair lift beside this last mountain section of the walk, and Valbione is also connected to Ponte di Legno - or, more exactly, the reverse is true - by chair lift. In summer it is invariably the case in my experience that the lifts are being oiled and greased on the day you arrive. Take heart, you wanted to walk anyway, so take Route 41 the short distance down into Ponte di Legno.

As mentioned above there is transport from Ponte back to Vezza, but those wishing to complete the round journey on foot should look out for the signs

Adamello and Presanella

for Route 10 close to the bottom station of the chair lift. The track here follows the old Roman road along the Via Valeriana, the first road ever built into this northern wilderness. The walk to Vezza takes about 2 hours, and is interesting all along its length, not only for its historical connections but for views to the high hills, and the fine stretches of woodland along its length.

Lake Garda

At 370 square kilometres (145 square miles), Lake Garda is the largest of the Italian lakes, even though its length, 52 kilometres ($32^1/_2$ miles), is considerably shorter than that of Lake Maggiore. The lake, shaped like an upturned hand axe, was carved by the Garda glacier which bit deepest at the northern end, where it was most confined by mountains, the water there being 342 metres (1,120 feet) deep. The mountains that confined the glacier now confine the lake. To the east is the long limestone ridge of Monte Baldo, beyond which is the Adige valley linking Trento and Verona. To the west there are even now cliffs with their feet in water. At its wider, southern, end the lake melts into the Lombardy plain, its drainage river, the Mincio meandering off from Peschiera to the Po.

Most visitors to the lake are attracted to its southern end, and to Sirmione. The town is reached along a narrow tongue of land poking out into the lake, about 3 kilometres (around 2 miles) long and narrowing to just 120 metres (400 feet) wide in places. Eventually drivers must leave their cars and walk to the town, all but essential vehicles being banned from the island town.

But though the bridge takes the visitor to the town, it feels as though you are actually entering the Scaligeri castle, which dominates the view rightwards. The Scaligeri built both the castle and the town walls in the 15th century when they were lords of Verona. Inside, the enchanting castle retains the machinery for a drawbridge, and the near perfect preservation of the upper battlements allows a good idea to be had of the method of protection, by sentinel post and removable foot-bridges.

The castle also includes on embattled quay. When in use, with oared galleys coming in from the lake, their assisting sails colourful against the blue waters, the castle must have been a splendid place, though perhaps not so when the Inquisitor of Mantua had 100 heretics burnt here.

On its eastern shore the road that takes the visitor along Lake Garda appears to have a continuous beach on one side and a tourist village on the other (with the notable exception of Malcesine, a wonderful village). The walker will be interested in this eastern shore because of Monte Baldo, a high and accessible ridge famous for its plant life.

Elsewhere, the lake is a little disappointing, and suffers from the closeness of the Brenta Dolomites just a little to the north. There are however, as we shall see, worthwhile outings on the west side where a series of high plateaux, some good isolated peaks and fine valleys offer excellent opportunities.

Walk 26 Colomber and Monte Pizzocolo

Map No:	KOMPASS Carta Turistica (1:50,000) Sheet 102 (Lago di Garda - Monte Baldo)
Walking Time:	6 hours
Grade:	Difficult
Highest Altitude:	Monte Pizzocolo 1,582m (5,189 feet)
Lowest Altitude:	Colomber 450m (1,476 feet)

Salò, a small town set in a square bay cut into the western shore of Lake Garda, has a strange position in the history of Italy. It is famous as the home of Gasparo da Salò, the man credited with the invention of the violin. A statue to the great man can be seen on the first floor of the 16th century Palazzo Municipale, the Town Hall. Several centuries later Salò was famous again, but briefly, towards the end of the 1939-45 War. With the invasion of Italy having been successfully completed, the Allies pushing rapidly northward through the country and the Italian partisans in control of much of the north, Hitler installed Mussolini as head of the Republic of Salò, a Fascist regime with its capital here on Lake Garda. The "Republic" did not last long and Mussolini was soon being evacuated to Germany. In fact he reached only as far as Dongo on the western shore of Lake Como before he was discovered by the partisans and executed.

Close to Salò are the resort towns of Gardone Riviera and Toscolano-Maderno. The former is home of the Hruska Botanical Gardens, one of Italy's finest gardens with over 2,000 species of plant, including what is widely believed to be Europe's finest rock gardens. Here too is the Vittoriale of the Italian poet-soldier Gabriele d'Annunzio, a friend of Mussolini and infamous for having taken the town of Fiume (now Rijeka in Yugoslavia) with a private army after the 1914-18 War had failed to deliver Istria to Italy as d'Annunzio believed was appropriate.

The Walk

The walk is straightforward if strenuous using mule tracks and military roads

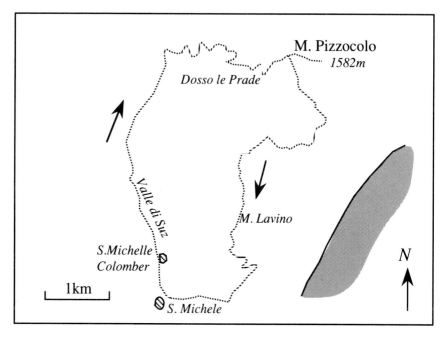

M. Pizzocolo
1582m

Dosso le Prade

Valle di Suz

M. Lavino

S.Michelle
Colomber

1km

S. Michele

N

throughout. It is at its best in the spring, from April until June, when the flowers are blooming, and in September and October when autumn's colours add to the views.

From Salò go to Gardone Riviera and take the road through S Michele to Colomber. Take the narrow lane beside River Besbesano (Route 1) that goes up the Valle di Suz, passing several very pretty houses on the 4 kilometre (2 mile) route to Verghere, where there is another car park. Continue on Route 1 which takes the wide mule track northward. This is a fine walk, crossing the stream several times - over delightful wooden bridges - and entering the Val Lataro near a collection of small waterfalls. The path leaves the stream, climbing up over pasture by way of several long bends, with fine views northward to Monte Spino, to reach Malga Gemelle. A malga is a dairy farm, and often the farmer will offer milk for sale. At Gemelle there is a fork in the track: go left on the steep track that reaches the Rifugio Pirlo allo Spino.

From the Rifugio, where there is also a chapel, a narrow road leads to the Passo dello Spino, at 1,160 metres (3,804 feet) passing an array of military buildings. Take Route 5 from the pass, a section of road called Via delle Merle, that goes into the woodland on the northern side of the Prade before climbing up to the western ridge of Monte Pizzocolo. Ignore the sign to the right for Route 13/S Urbano - we will be going to that small village, but not by that route. Our descent route will be Route 11, passed further on. Ahead is Dosso (rising ridge) delle Prade from which a mule track leads under the summit of Monte Pizzocolo, passing the ruins of some old military buildings to reach a fork near a small pool. Stay with the mule track, which goes right, Route 11, up the final slopes to the summit of Monte Pizzocolo with its cross. From the summit there are beautiful views, virtually the whole of Lake Garda being visible. Across the lake is the long chain of Monte Baldo, while to the north are the peaks of the Adamello, the Brenta and Ortles-Cevedale Alps. To the west, away from the lake, are the pre-Alps of the Brescia and Bergamo valleys, while to the south across the Lombardy Plain are the Apennines.

Reverse the final ascent and go west back to the signed (Route 11) going south down the Valle della Prera. The track passes the Malga Valle and soon after, in the woods beyond, there is a collection of giasere caves, caves where winter's snows were packed to form ice that lasted through the summer and was used to refrigerate food in the villages at the base of the hill. Route 11 leaves the valley path after about 800 metres ($^1/_2$ mile), going west to the Casotto dei Veronesi, a shelter and then going steeply down to reach a road. Go right for about 700 metres to S Urbano with its small chapel. From the end of the village go left on a track beneath a tiny villa (Cecaetoa) and past several more. Look for the sign G2: follow the path it indicates, with an expanding view of Monte Baldo and Lake Garda. The track reaches Buelimo, continuing towards and then around to the right (west) of Monte Lavino (907 metres - 2,975 feet). At a fork go left to reach a road near the farmhouse of Casadur in Lavino Inferiore.

The road ahead falls steeply to a junction. Go right to reach S Michele. At the school go right between houses and then take steps down to another road near the Ferdinando bridge (Ponte Ferdinando) and go north from there back to Colomber.

Walk 27   Magasa and Monte Caplone

Map No:	KOMPASS Carta Turistica (1:50,000)
	Sheet 102 (Lago di Garda - Monte Baldo)
Walking Time:	6 hours
Grade:	Difficult
Highest Altitude:	Monte Caplone 1,976m (6,481 feet)
Lowest Altitude:	Magasa 981m (3,218 feet)

Between Lake Garda and Lake Idro the country is high and mountainous, the mountains split by deep valleys. Of these valleys the largest is Valvestino, a valley with its own large lake. At the head of the valley is a wall of peaks, the highest of which is Monte Caplone. Our walk climbs this peak, using Magasa, the biggest high valley village, as a start point.

The Walk

Magasa is reached from Gargnano, on Lake Garda's western shore, by way of Valvestino, a village that shares its name with the valley. Our route from it follows mule tracks and old military roads, and is waymarked throughout with red paint flashes.

The route leaves the village along the main street, bearing left to reach a fountain, past the War Memorial, then go right on the mule track that climbs the steep side of the valley. The track goes past a small chapel and then reaches the tiny village of Pilaster (1,271 metres - 4,169 feet). Bear right on the village road for 600 metres to reach a mule track to the left. Follow this to a fork, after another 600 metres, where you go right. The track crosses a bridge, beyond which is the Grune, an upland area between valley streams, the best of the rock outcrops on it being the Rocca Pagana, a sharp, angular block that the route goes above. From the Grune ridge there are fine views down the Valvestino to Magasa and the mountains beyond.

Look out on the right for a track going to the Rifugio Cima Rest: this is the return route we shall follow. For the moment though we bear left on the well signed track heading northward towards the valley's imposing back wall. The

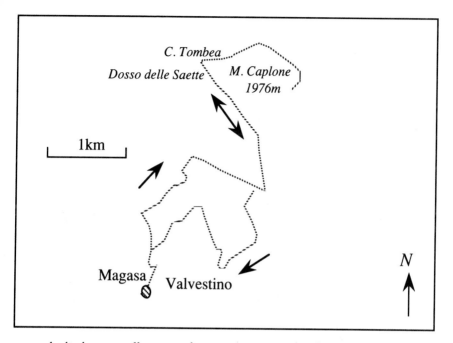

C. Tombea

Dosso delle Saette

M. Caplone
1976m

1km

Magasa

Valvestino

N

track climbs now, offering good views across towards Pilaster and the early part of the walk. Closer at hand there are rock outcrops and, beyond a little stream, the remnants of some trenches dug during the 1914-18 War. It is a odd sight: why were they thinking of fighting here, in such difficult to reach country? The answer will be obvious a little further along the route.

Beyond the trenches an old military road takes the walker up to meet a mule track that once connected the Bocca di Caplone with the Bocca di Lorina. Bear right on this track towards the Malga (Alpine Hut) Tombea, set in a wide, green plain, but before reaching it go right on another mule track, one used, and repaired, during the war and follow it as it winds its way up to Cima Tombea (at 1,950 metres - 6,396 feet), a top with an incongruous mixture of war ruins and beautiful alpine flowers, good in both spring and summer. From the summit there is a wide view, with lakes Garda and Idro being visible, as well as the snowy tops of the Adamello and the rocky mass of the Brenta.

The slightly higher summit of Monte Caplone is reached by a track that goes down to the big Bocca di Campei (1822 metres - 5,976 feet) by way of a tunnel through the rock. Ignore the mule track going down left to Bocca di Lorina, continuing on the obvious track to the top. Monte Caplone is also known as Cima delle Guardie - the Peak of the Guards because, until 1918,

Valvestino

it was on the border between Italy and Austria. That is why the Italian entrenched the flat lands below the peak.

From the top go back down to Bocca di Campei and reverse the route down past Malga Tombea and the Valle di Campei to reach the little track, now on the left, past on the outward journey. Bear left down this to reach a second alpine hut, Malga Alvezza (1,280 metres - 4,198 feet). Beyond the track crosses the Prati di Rest, a fine alp - an upland grassy plain - to reach the Rifugio Rest set close to other houses.

Follow the metalled from the hamlet and, near the chapel, take the track on the right that cuts a off a bend, falling sharply to rejoin the road. Go right to reach the bridge at Castello, under the Rocca Pagana, beyond which the road is followed back to Magasa.

Walk 28   Limone sul Garda

Map No:	KOMPASS Carta Turistica (1:50,000) Sheet 102 (Lago di Garda - Monte Baldo)
Walking Time:	6 hours
Grade:	Difficult
Highest Altitude:	Punta di Mois 1,376m (4,513 feet)
Lowest Altitude:	Limone sul Garda 66m (216 feet)

Mid-way, but perhaps a little further north than that, along the western shore of Lake Garda are two high plateaux hewn out of the rock of the pre-Alps. These are Tremosine and Tignale, and they are among the most beautiful areas on the lake's shore with green meadows and tall rock faces, and little, picturesque villages. Below Tremosine is Limone, named for the lemon trees that were planted here for the first time in Europe, and which still grow here together with oranges, mandarins and olives. Limone has a delightful old quarter, close to the old port, where houses with window boxes are piled high upon each other. And at its northern end are the cliffs of Cima Mughera, gleaming white except where the plant life, in more shades of green than can be described, clings. Our route climbs Cima Mughera, and visits Tremosine, taking the walker through an area known as *dei fortini* because of the old barracks and fortifications left over from the 1914-18 War, as well as the wild valley of Singol.

The Walk

The Gardesana Occidentale (the road along the western shore of Lake Garda, the SS45) cuts through the western edge of Limone, passing close to the church. Find the church and cross the main road. The Via Caldogno leaves the small square here: take it and follow it to its end from where a track bordered on the left by a stream, the Torrente S Giovanni, leads to a bridge over the stream used to reach a wide mule track going up the Valle del Singol. Follow the track, signed for Route 101, passing several excellent small waterfalls and, on the left, Route 102 that goes up in the Valle Scaglione.

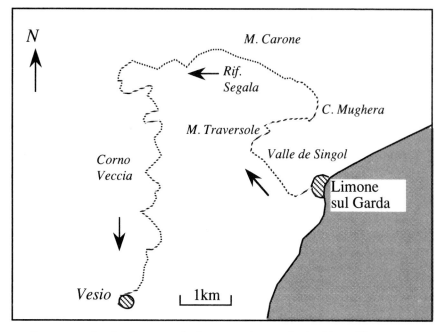

Cross a wooden bridge to reach the ruins of a circular building. The stream is crossed again, beyond which a series of bends leads to the Madonnina (little Madonna) del Murel set on the rocks to the left. Ahead now is the Ranzo fork where the mule track goes straight on (Route 103) but we go right on Route 101 through a superb wood then up Val Salumi, assisted by another series of bends.

The route passes below the summit of Cima di Mughera (1161 metres - 3,808 feet), but it can be comfortably reached by a small diversion. From the top the view is beautiful, taking in the northern part of Lake Garda, with Monte Baldo and other surrounding mountains.

Route 101 now reaches the prominent Roccolo di Nembra from where we take Route 422 along the obvious mule track that has come up, from the right, from Pregasina, a hamlet close to Riva del Garda. The mule track goes left, soon reaching Passo Guil (at 1,209 metres - 3,966 feet) where it joins another mule track, taken by Route 424, coming from Pre in the Val di Ledro. Bear left again, passing around the Punta di Mois and soon reaching Baite Bartolomeo Segala (at 1,250 metres - 4,100 feet) where there is a very pleasant little church. From the hut take Route 421, on a wide track which is now followed for some distance, passing several more old barrack buildings and, to the right, Route 105, which is heading off to the summit of Monte

Carone. Continue over the Passo di Bestana (at 1,274 metres - 4,179 feet) but before reaching the Passo Nota cross a bridge on the left following signs for the Cimitero di Guerra (War Cemetery) and a sign for Route 121. Follow the wide track to a small clearing where, to the left, you can visit the evocative little cemetery, recently restored by the folk of Vesio di Tremosine. It is a strange spot for such a place, the sadder somehow for being surrounded by such beauty. Those who lie here died to maintain this place as a part of Italy.

Continue along the high northern side of Valle delle Cerese to reach a fork where Route 102 is signed to the right. Follow the route as it meanders beneath Monte Traversole. This is an old military road, the views from which, of the Valle di Bondo and the tops of Tremalzo are wonderful. After 1¹/₂ kilometres (1 mile) leave Route 102, taking Route 106 on the right, a track that goes through five tunnels as it burrows its way through wildly beautiful country beneath the Corno delle Vecchia. Beyond the fifth tunnel the track widens as it passes below Corno Nero (1402 m). Continue beneath the Punta della Brosa Cima della Selva - the latter a fine viewpoint at 1,281 metres (4,202 feet) that can be easily reached by a mule track to the left of our track.

The track is now in fine country, traversing below the Cima Sospir, the Bocca dei Sospiri and Dalvra Alta. After this last peak the track descends around many bends to the Piazzale (little square) G. Angelini on the outskirts of Vesio, where a plaque under the cypresses remembers the local forestry worker. A track from the square runs parallel to the Valle di Bondo road, reaching a crossroads with the road from Vesio (Hotel Le Balze) to Campi. Here go right to reach Vesio centre along Via Orsino.

Vesio is one of the biggest and most pleasant hamlets of Tremosine, and from it buses run back to Limone sul Garda.

Walk 29   On Top of Monte Baldo

Map No:	KOMPASS Carta Turistica (1:50,000) Sheet 102 (Lago di Garda - Monte Baldo)
Walking Time:	4 hours
Grade:	Medium, but with a difficult final section
Highest Altitude:	Cima Valdritta 2,218m (7,275 feet)
Lowest Altitude:	Tratto Spin 1,750m (5,740 feet)

Malcesine is among the most famous towns on Lake Garda, not least for its impressive Scaligeri castle, a huge almost complete building perched right at the lake edge, and with a tall square central tower that dominates the town from any direction. The castle, built in the early 14th century, houses the Museum of the Lake and among the exhibits are models and drawings of the transportation of Venetian war galleys to Torbole. The galleys were rowed up river from Venice, then dragged across country in dis-assembled form, rebuilt at Torbole and launched to help the Venetian Republic take control of Lake Garda. The phenomenal effort was fruitless: the Venetians lost a battle on the lake.

A walk within the town almost qualifies for this book, and you should certainly not miss the 15th century Palazzo dei Capitani - the palace of the Venetian Captains of the Lake near the harbour - which is now the Town Hall, a most impressive building with its pillars and arcaded windows. Do not miss the view across to the tiny Island of Olives and be sure also to find the inscribed stone headed -

HINC

J.W. GOETHE

ARCEM DELINEAVAT

because there can be few towns anywhere that have raised a memorial to an arrest. The arrest occurred on 13th September 1786 when Johann Wolfgang Goethe visited Italy for the first time. At that time the border between Austria and Italy lay between Torbole and Malcesine, so on present day terms Goethe was already in Italy as he made his way from one town to the other.

In Malcesine he was, as we have been, impressed by the castle, and paused to sketch it. He was seen, and promptly arrested as an Austrian spy, having no small difficulty in proving his innocence as a citizen of the Republic of Frankfurt. When he was released the great man saw the funny side of it all, writing a humorous account in his "Italian Tour".

Behind the town rises Monte Baldo, sometimes known as the "Botanical Garden of Italy" for the profusion of both species and growth, and the rarity of some plants, on its flanks. Two Natural Parks have been set up on the mountain to preserve the flora, and the insects, birds and animals. The Selva Pezzi Park is high on the peak, one boundary running along the ridge through the highest tops, the other lying on the flank above Malcesine. The Gardesana Orientale Park lies above the lakeside road from Malcesine to Torbole. The walk described here lies within the Selva Pezzi Park. It goes without saying that the collecting of specimens from within the Park is forbidden.

The Walk

From Malcesine take the cable car to Tratto Spin - on the Monte Baldo ridge at 1,750 metres (5,740 feet) - a journey of about 15 minutes which saves several hours of climbing. From the top station - where there are hotels and restaurants - there is a tremendous panorama across the lake and towards the high peaks of the Adamello and the Brenta, as well as of the local tops of Monte Baldo itself. Looking down to Malcesine the range of vegetation is remarkable. At the lakeside are olive trees, looking like a real section of wood from here. Then comes natural woodland, firstly dark firs, then beech and spruce, all intermingled with alp (pasture) dotted with alpine huts.

Close to the top station are the ski-lifts of Garda's foremost winter sport area. Go south along the ridge between these, the path passing through flourishing rhododendron bushes and soon reaching the first bare rocks. The first top, Cima delle Pozzette (2,132 metres - 6,993 feet) is reached after about one hour's walking. This is the north top of Monte Baldo that, from the lakeside, dominates the farmland of Artillone and the Val Angual. It is a good viewpoint: to the north is Altissimo, the extreme end of Baldo chain, the rocky terrace of Corna Piana and Brentonico valley.

Continue along the ridge, passing Cima del Longino (2,180 metres - 7,150 feet) and Cima di Val Finestra (2,079 metres - 6,819 feet). Ahead now the ridge path goes to the left (east) of the highest point, though the top itself can be reached on a short, but tricky path. Be cautious here, going no further than you feel is safe. Remember that you will have to come back. The compensation

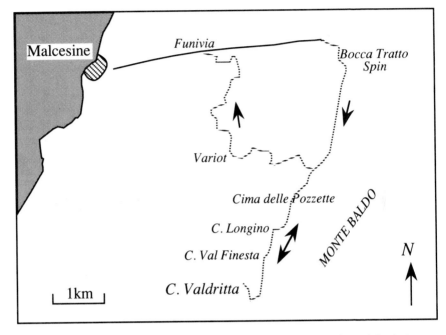

is, of course, standing on Cima Valdritta, at 2,218 metres (7,275 feet) the highest point on the Monte Baldo ridge.

The final section of the ridge path towards Cima Valdritta, and especially the more sheltered hill sections to the side of the ridge, are carpeted with alpine flowers in Spring and Summer. Here too the lucky (?) walker may see an asp viper. Be cautious if you do: these snakes are a really lucky find and you will be pleased to have seen one, but they are more dangerous than the British adder and should not be approached.

From Cima Valdritta the ridge can be followed southward, but the going becomes increasingly difficult. Monte Maggiore, the next big peak, is not at all easy to reach, the extension to it requiring time, as well as some climbing experience.

To return to Malcesine, reverse the route to the top station or, for a more active variation, take the path that goes down the Val Bona (that is, westward) from the col beyond (that is, to the north of) Cima delle Pozzette. The path here extends the view by offering one across the face of the Monte Baldo high peaks, and crosses more flower-laden ground. It goes steeply down to reach the forest station at the Col di Piombi (at 1,158 metres - 3,798 feet) close to excellent forests of spruce and pale fir. From the Col a mule track leads to the intermediate station of the funivia. It is arguable whether the

On Monte Baldo

walker is better off spending time on this descent or in a more detailed exploration of the high ridge.

Walk 30   At the Foot of Monte Baldo

Map No:	KOMPASS Carta Turistica (1:50,000) Sheet 102 (Lago di Garda - Monte Baldo)
Walking Time:	4 hours
Grade:	Easy
Highest Altitude:	Prada Alta 1,000m (3,280 feet)
Lowest Altitude:	Marniga 90m (295 feet)

The section of Lake Garda's coast around Malcesine is known as the Riviera of Olives and this low lying walk on the flank of Monte Baldo goes through, and offers views to, some of the olive plantations. It follows mule tracks, no longer used by the muleteers as they were when the tracks were the trade routes of the area, but still used by local farmers to move their stock, or to collect firewood. The start point is Marniga, a tiny village that part of the locality of Brenzone. As Marniga can also be reached by bus from Malcesine (see Walk 29), as can the village of Castelletto that is reached by an alternative ending, it is perhaps better to use that town as a start point, to ease the parking problems.

The Walk

Start from the little square in the village of Marniga and take the old mule track that rises steeply between the houses before levelling out between gardens and fields. In about 15 minutes you reach Campo, an old village - it was built in the Middle Ages and once boasted a castle - but now almost abandoned, the total number of inhabitants being no more than ten. There is a spring in the village, the best (only) refreshment being the clear water it provides. Go through the village, noticing the occasional millstone still visible, a memento of the time when the village was rich from the efforts of its millers as well as the farmers and fisherfolk. The mule track goes up behind the church, passing a few solitary trees before reaching a wood. The valley here was cut by an Ice Age glacier, some of the boulders showing evidence of its cutting edge.

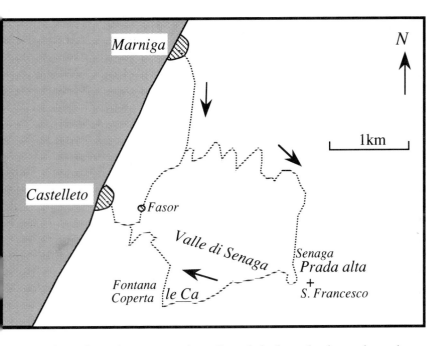

As the mule track zig-zags up the valley side look out for the marks made by the sledges loaded with wood or other odds and ends that were drawn behind the mules. Look too for the iron hooks used by the muleteers to hold the load while the mule rested or, sometimes, to take a rope so the man could help his animals. Continue climbing, passing the first chestnut trees, to reach the green and wild Prada Alta, a flat land at about 1,000 metres (3,280 feet) from where there is a beautiful view of Monte Baldo.

When a road is reached go right along it (towards S Zeno di Montagna), passing the church of S Francesco to the left after about 800 metres ($^1/_2$ mile). About 200 metres further on take the track on the right. The track soon reaches a balcon (balcony) from where the view of the lake and of nearby Valle Senaga is excellent. Beyond the lake are the mountains of Val Sabbia and Val Camonica, Monte Pizzocolo standing out especially well. This peak - sometimes called the Nose of Napoleon (!) - is climbed on Walk 26. Far to the right of the peak are the upland regions of Tignale and Tremosine.

The mule track descends quickly from the balcony reaching a pool and a small chestnut tree wood close to La Ca. Continue to Fontana Coperta where there is a welcome spring, elegantly enclosed. Cross the road beyond the spring into an area of trees and shrubs and go down to the hamlet of Biasa where the first refreshment stop of the walk is available (other than the

Malcesine and Monte Baldo

springwater of course). From the village there is a choice: go ahead, down the road to Castelletto from where a bus can be used to return to Marniga; or, and better, go along the road to Fasor and through that village to reach a track - to the left as the road swings sharply right - for Campo. From there, reverse the outward route to Marniga.